What People Are Saying About
Teens Talkin' Faith . . .

"Teens Talkin' Faith is a great book for all teens, even if you doubt God. There were several passages from teens that I could relate to and that let me know I am not the only one who has certain thoughts or doubts about God."

Amanda, 15

"This book will completely soothe your soul!"

Liz, 14

"Teens Talkin' Faith touched me because it helped me to know that kids like me pray to God for courage. The teens who wrote for this book inspired me to look to God when I am feeling sad or lonely and to remember that God will always be with me."

David, 15

"This book is an assurance to teens, to let them know that there are others who feel the same way they do about their beliefs and struggles with God. We will use it as a companion to teach teens who are searching for the light of Christ."

Keith and Nicole Lewis
youth ministers

"As far as I am concerned, Mrs. T was sent here by God to share His love and compassion with us and to help us, as teens, find our way. Thanks, Mrs. T!"

Ian, 17

"Every time I read Mrs. T's words or hear her speak, she reaches a place in my heart that I never knew I had!"

͞ ͞an, 16

"Mrs. T's *Teens Talkin' F͞*   know
that other teens who re͞   I do!"

di, 15

D1316182

TEENS TALKIN' FAITH

A Christian Perspective

Written and Compiled by

Michelle L. Trujillo

954-360-7204

954-360-0909

HCI TEENS™

Health Communications, Inc.
Deerfield Beach, Florida

www.hci-online.com

Library of Congress Cataloging-in-Publication Data

Trujillo, Michelle L., date.
    Teens talkin' faith : a Christian perspective / written and
compiled by Michelle Trujillo.
       p.   cm.
    ISBN 1-55874-941-1 (trade paper)
    1. Teenagers—Religious life. I. Title.

    BV4447 .T77 2001
    248.8'3—dc21

                                      2001039300

©2001 Michelle L. Trujillo
ISBN 1-55874-941-1

Publisher: Health Communications, Inc.
               3201 S.W. 15th Street
               Deerfield Beach, FL 33442-8190

Cover and inside design by Lisa Camp
Inside formatting by Dawn Grove

This book is dedicated to

My parents, Gary and Judy Williams

*Is there a greater gift that parents can give
their child than that of faith?*

*You have filled my life with love and
shown me faith through your example.
I love you both.*

And

In memory of

My grandfather, Robert E. Williams

*Who blessed my life with lessons of humility,
wisdom and integrity.*

*I love you, Bapa, and I'll carry your smile
in my heart always!*

Contents

Acknowledgments ix

Author's Note xi

CHAPTER ONE: Faith! 1

CHAPTER TWO: Am I the Only One
Who Doubts God? 31

CHAPTER THREE: God, Grant Me Courage 69

CHAPTER FOUR: You Are My Strength! 105

CHAPTER FIVE: In You I Trust! 141

CHAPTER SIX: God, How Could You
Let This Happen?! 173

CHAPTER SEVEN: How Can You Forgive Me
After What I Have Done? 203

CHAPTER EIGHT: Hey God, Can You
Hear Me Way Up There? 239

CHAPTER NINE: I Love You, Lord! 281

CHAPTER TEN: Let Me Share Your Hope 319

Note to the Reader 361

Appendix I: Scriptural References 363

Appendix II: Resources and Hotlines 379

Acknowledgments

This book would not have become a reality without the input, insight and inspiration of so many people. I would especially like to thank the following:

First and foremost, God! His presence joined me on the spiritual journey that became *Teens Talkin' Faith.* I thank You and praise You, Lord, for Your inspiration and Your love. Through You, I know that all things *are* possible!

My husband, David. Your love gives me strength; your humility touches my heart. I thank God for blessing me so richly with your love! Thank you for the time you spent editing this book and helping me to be a better writer. . . . And to our children. You fill my life with joy!

Eileen Decker and Joanne Kortan. You saved me (and my back)! Thank you.

The staff at HCI, especially Lisa Drucker and Susan Tobias. I feel blessed to work with you both! Thank you for your editing expertise, compassion and for letting teens have a say in how the book was designed and developed. Peter Vegso, thanks for giving this book an opportunity to touch teens! Erica Orloff, you make the editing process insightful and fun! Thank you for your knowledge and encouragement.

Joe Gorton, Brandy Rapley, Laura Peterson and the Rauber family. Thank you for letting me share your stories. And to Amanda, Sarah, Sion, Courtney and Jason, too. I appreciate you all!

All of those who provided spiritual counsel and prayers, especially the pastors, priests and youth leaders with whom I consulted, and my mom Judy Williams, Janell Sheets and Father Warren Savage, as well as friends and family who supported me throughout the process.

And last, but definitely not least, to all of the teens who contributed to this book. Thank you for sharing your hearts and your lives. This book would not have become a reality without you. Thanks also to the many teachers and principals who allowed their students to write. Thank you all!

Author's Note

While writing this book, I tried to put myself in your shoes. I realized that you may be incredibly strong in your faith and committed to Christianity. On the other hand, you may be struggling with your spiritual beliefs and looking for answers. Perhaps you are not a Christian but open to learning about this faith. Regardless, I pray that wherever you are on your spiritual journey, you will keep an open mind and allow the words written on these pages to touch your heart.

Furthermore, please understand that this is not a book about religion. It is, instead, about accepting and building a relationship with God through your life experiences as a teen. My personal contributions are written from a Christian perspective. However, teens throughout the nation from all ethnic, socioeconomic and religious backgrounds also contributed. It is important for you to know that the thoughts and beliefs of these teens do not directly reflect my thoughts and beliefs as the author. They also may not coincide with your personal ideas or opinions. So please, take them for the individual life experiences and spiritual perspectives that they are.

In addition, please know that I have changed all of the

names of the teen contributors, as well as a few of their ages, in order to protect their privacy and that of their friends and family. When needed, context, and less frequently, content, was modified for the protection of those involved and to contribute to the continuity of each chapter.

The format of this book was designed with the input of teens like you. Each chapter of *Teens Talkin' Faith* begins with an introduction or brief excerpt from me, Mrs. T, as I am known to most teens. This is followed by a collection of writings from teen contributors. Every chapter concludes with a "T" Talk, again written by me. I use the "T" Talks to summarize each chapter with personal stories, spiritual insight and inspirational guidance.

Finally, know that I wrote *Teens Talkin' Faith* to honor God and bring His hope to you, as a teenager. I pray that this book will lead you on a spiritual journey that will enrich your faith and draw you closer to God.

CHAPTER ONE

Faith!

Just for starters, let's talk about faith . . .

At fifteen, Brandy was presumably a lot like you or some of your friends. She was a star athlete and incredibly social. Brandy hung with the "in" crowd and didn't have many worries. Her world revolved around school, friends, sports and occasional parties. It was after one such party that Brandy's world was shattered. On the way home from this party, the truck she was riding in was hit by another vehicle and rolled three times. Ironically, out of the five people involved in the accident, Brandy was the only one badly injured and the only one not drinking that night.

Brandy was left unconscious in the cab of the pickup while the others escaped to safety. Unaware that the truck would ignite, her friends were more concerned about staying out of trouble than

rescuing Brandy. They either left the scene or scur-
ried about trying to hide all evidence of their under-
aged drinking. While they were scattering beer cans,
Brandy was burning.

Over 75 percent of Brandy's body and most of
her face was burned before a brave young man
pulled her free from the hot flames. She lost her
soft, smooth skin and her pretty hair. She lost her
right ear, a finger on her right hand and her entire
left arm. Brandy lost her spot on the all-star softball team and her "normal" teen life of flirting with
guys and hanging with friends.

In an instant, Brandy's life as a teenager changed.
For many teens, appearance is extremely important.
Acceptance is paramount. How teens look, dress or
what they are involved in can often determine their
sense of belonging among their peers. Think about
yourself. Are your looks important to you? Do you
play any sports or a musical instrument? Are you
involved in any clubs or after-school activities?
Considering your life, can you imagine stepping into
Brandy's shoes? Picture yourself so badly disfig-
ured that you are no longer recognizable.
Contemplate the changes you would have to make in
your day-to-day activities if you lost one of your
arms. Suppose you were the one left in that burning
truck. Could you survive the pain, isolation and

such extreme change? Would you even want to?

When I heard about Brandy, my initial response was to whisper to God, "Why, why did this have to happen? How can one girl go through so much?" But Brandy is able to see beyond my prevailing questions. Her faith has made her strong. A few years after her accident, Brandy and I became friends. The first time we ever spoke, she told me that she thanked God for her life today. She also astounded me with her wisdom when she said, "I don't blame God. Really, if I blame anyone, I blame myself because I was there. I chose to go to the party. I knew that the driver of the truck I was riding in had been drinking, and I chose to put myself in that situation." However, Brandy understands that placing blame on herself, God or the others involved in the accident has no benefit. So instead, she acknowledges with gratefulness that she has evolved as a person and that her life has significant purpose. Yet that realization is not one that she came to readily. It was a slow awakening.

Five months after the accident and two days before her sixteenth birthday, Brandy was released from the hospital. Once home, she wanted to hang with friends and be a "regular" teen again. Although Brandy physically looked like a different person, inside she was still the same. This was very painful for Brandy because even her friends, initially, felt awkward. Like so many other people, they stared. So, when she went out with friends, she made decisions to drink and to be sexually promiscuous. Brandy struggled with the reasons why she made these choices, especially after all she had been through. Yet, she tested herself and her faith because she wanted to be "in," she wanted to be accepted.

Eventually, Brandy came to realize that many of the decisions she made after the accident were an attempt to prove to herself and her friends that nothing had changed and that she was still the same person. However, each time she participated in risky behavior, she knew it wasn't right. Slowly, Brandy grasped the notion that she didn't want to be the person she was before her accident. She realized that she used to be snobby, sometimes even rude to people. Her relationship with her mother was tense and argumentative. They didn't get along or do much together. At the time, Brandy felt that appearance was important and faith was insignificant. But now, Brandy cared more about people. She began to appreciate her mom, and they became closer than ever. She also came to understand that looks, in fact, don't matter. Instead, she learned that it is who you are inside that truly counts.

Brandy began to cherish her relationships and value her faith.

As she looked back, Brandy realized the constants in her life were her family, close friends and faith. Furthermore, she began to see that her faith, a treasure she often overlooked, was the strength that pulled her through. From the very beginning, when Brandy arrived by care flight at the hospital with her skin melted and charred, her mom asked her, "Is God with you?" Although she was really "out of it" and couldn't talk, Brandy nodded her head, "Yes, God is here." And even before that, as she lay in the midst of flames, a young man named Jimmy attempted to pull her free. He tried and tried until he didn't think he could pull anymore, but God was there. In a final effort, with a silent request for help, Jimmy says that Brandy floated out of that truck as light as a feather. And following her recovery, Brandy knows that God was with her when she made poor decisions by helping her ultimately to choose the right paths. Brandy believes that if you ask God for help, He will help you. Through right or wrong, trial or suffering, He is there.

Throughout this book you will find God's presence. Within these pages, as teens share their confusion and doubts, struggles and fears, triumphs and hopes, they will also share their faith.

Regardless of where you reside spiritually at this
point in your life, I pray that when you read this
book, you allow God to embrace your heart.

Teens Talkin' Faith will lead you to discover unconditional love and help you to find peace in
your life. It is a journey of faith toward God that will
lead you to this discovery. If you are already strong
in your religious convictions, then you may know
what I am talking about. Perhaps you have experienced the feeling of peace that enters your life
when you turn to God for guidance or solace.
Likely, you have felt the joy that fills your heart
when you focus on the Lord. You don't need drugs,
alcohol or sex to find happiness as a teenager. You
can find it in God. However, I'm sure that you know
there is always room for spiritual growth.

On the other hand, if faith has never been a part
of your life, then I am very excited to share the glory
of God with you. My message in this book is enthu-
siastically simple. God cares! You can flee to Him for
comfort. You can rely on Him for unconditional love.
I want you to know that God is available and waiting
for you to call on Him. He is there to guide, support
and, as He did for Brandy, provide courage and
strength. His patience is plentiful, and His forgiveness is given freely. As a teen you may experience
small traumas in your life or painful tragedies like

Brandy's. You may feel, sometimes, that you are all alone. But you are not. God is always there. Often, it is just a matter of opening your heart to His presence.

When you invite God into your life, His spirit will fill your heart. He is not a God who reigns from heaven demanding perfection and punishing anything less. Instead, He is someone with whom you can have a relationship. He is a God who loves you completely, with all of your faults and insecurities. You can talk to Him every day, every moment, because He always has time. God also inspired an awesome book that you can turn to for guidance and direction. It is the Bible, and it was written for you to foster your relationship with God and help you to live a life full of joy and hope.

You might be thinking, "Yeah, that sounds great, but how do I know God is really there?" The answer is faith. What is faith? Faith is believing without actually seeing. It is relying on your heart instead of your head. Faith is letting go of the tough stuff in your life and turning it over to God, looking to Him for guidance and direction. Amazingly, faith is knowing in the depths of your soul that you are God's child and that He will take care of you.

Many teen contributors expressed that by writing for this book, their faith grew. I hope that by reading this book your faith will grow, too. Like Brandy, you may experience trials or hardships in your life, but faith can help you to persevere. Brandy said that after her accident she never wanted to give up. "I got a second chance," she said. "I am not going to sit here and waste what God has given me. I kind of feel like it was meant to be this way, like I am here for a reason." Her faith touched my life. Her wisdom opened my eyes. People often assume that you must be an adult to be wise. But after meeting Brandy and so many other teenagers, I know this isn't true. Wisdom can be born from experience. The teens who have written for this book share their experiences, doubts, wisdom and faith with you. I hope that you consider them your friends. Appreciate their experiences and take from each something that you can apply to your life. Find love, faith and hope on these pages. Find the Lord!

Mrs. T

God is my friend . . .

There are many people in life who believe in things, and they are not really sure why. Some believe because that was the way they were brought up. Then, there are those who believe in things because they know in their hearts that the thing they believe in truly exists. Well, that is how I feel about God. Although I have never physically seen Him, I know in my heart He is truly present and that He watches over me each and every day. I talk to Him every day, and I know He is listening to me when I speak. Even when I become upset with Him, I know His love for me is never ending, and my love for Him is the same. God is my friend, and these feelings we have for each other will never change.

Whit, 18

I pray to God every night and thank Him for my life . . .

I believe in God because He has helped me through my life. My mother is recovering from a drug addiction and alcoholism, and my father is a workaholic. Now I live with my grandparents. I pray to God every night and thank Him for my life, health and wonderful family. I am so lucky to have my two incredible grandparents to take care of me. I believe that God gives you strength when you need it, and He would never give you something you could not handle. He is always forgiving and helps me through the tough times. I believe that there is a God and He is looking out for each and every one of us. If you search really hard, you can feel the love of God through others. God is incredible and will never give up on you. All you have to do to find Him is reach out.

Clairesse, 15

He is always there . . .

People ask me all the time, "Why do you believe in God? You can't see Him." I have an answer. I see God all the time. I believe because God is available; He is there when I need Him. When I want Him to be somewhere, He is. I really turned to God during my first baseball season. I would stand on first base and all through the game keep looking for my dad. But he was never there. I was so disappointed, so I started to read my Bible and pray. I realized that hoping my dad would show was less and less important to me. I learned I could depend on God. He was always there. When He says He will do something, I know without a doubt He will. I know when I need comfort He will comfort me. It says in the Bible that God will never leave or forsake me. So He is the one I depend on. He is the only one I tell everything to. I am not afraid of what He will say nor will I be embarrassed since I know He won't ever leave or forsake me. My faith is so important because without God I would probably not have a clue as to how to go through my life. God is the reason I get up in the morning. And I have no worries. Death used to scare the crap out of me, but I no longer fear it. I know where I will go. I can't lecture people when they ask about God because I don't have all the answers, so who am I to lecture you? I believe wholeheartedly, though, that my God is awesome.

Analyn, 15

God is the best listener . . .

Why do I believe in God? Why do I believe in hope? God is someone to turn to and someone who will listen to me when I need help. God is the best listener I know, just as hope is a powerful cry that tells me life will always get better. One reason I love God is because He is all around me; He is in the sky, the birds and my family and friends. God works through them because of love. God is not just a last resort when no one can help you out: He is the one whose love is unconditional and can be received as your best friend. I believe that God helps us all and does not have favorites. He is the kindness in a stranger or the beauty of a spring day. He is love—love for all humanity and even for the little pebble on a dirt road. He loves all His creations because they are good. My faith is very important to me, but first I had to understand what faith is. Webster's Dictionary *defines faith as a belief in a revealed religion. I define faith as my trust and reverence in God. I have trust in God, as a bee trusts a flower not to toss it off. I have an unbreakable faith in my God because He loves me. He cares about me as me and not as a straight-A student, or a singer, or a son, but as myself. He is the one and only one who can do this. That is why I believe in God, because He cares and loves me as me.*

Dante, 18

God is someone you can look up to . . .

God is a good guy. He is cool. He does things for a good cause, and I believe in Him. Well, I mean, I am not one of these gung ho religious guys or anything, but I know He is there. It doesn't matter if you are Christian, Jewish, Muslim or even an atheist. He is still there in any form you choose to accept Him. That's why it irritates me when I go to church and all I hear is that my religion is the only one and that if you don't accept it you will burn in hell. This is my opinion, of course, but I think that is for God to judge. But I still believe in God, and I think everyone should. God is someone you can look up to, and someone you can trust. He is not a group you go to every Sunday to reaffirm your faith. Church is your responsibility, but God can be for you what He is for me—a relationship.

Vincent, 14

... no one is beyond hope

There are many reasons to believe in God. Perhaps, like myself, some are brought up in a surrounding of strong faith in God. But speaking in general, especially to teenagers, God can act as something more than a reason to get up on Sunday morning. In today's world, teens are in the direct line of the negative aspects that today's society is constantly putting in front of our faces—sex, drugs, alcohol and much, much more. They are all directly associated with teenagers, so I think it is safe to say that we are the generation that needs God the most. And sadly, I think we are also the ones who most often neglect Him. But no one is beyond hope. No matter how grave the sin, God will forgive in return for your love. That said, it is also certain to say that, no matter what way you view it, faith in God can answer many of your problems. If you live by God, morally and spiritually, no matter what your religious background, you can be a better person. The way God wants us to live should not be interpreted as perfection. God Himself, through scripture, stated that no man is perfect. The one thing He asks is that we try our best, our very hardest, to live in the image and likeness of God.

Martin, 16

Faith is important to me because . . .

I believe in God because I have no doubt in my
mind that a higher power exists. When I look
around me, there is so much goodness to be seen.
Everything in the world had to have been created and planned ahead of time. As people, we
do not simply appear on this Earth. Instead, God
places each and every one of us on this Earth for
a specific purpose and to fulfill the plan of God.
I personally feel God's presence around me in
times of difficulty. He lends His hand in times
when hope cannot be found. Faith is important
to me because I feel that faith is necessary in
order to build a healthy relationship with God. It
is important to have something to believe in, for
there is nothing greater than sharing in God's
love. I have heard that if you do not believe in
God during this life, and then you find that He
truly does exist, you have everything to lose. If

you do believe in God, and He does not exist, you have nothing to lose. And if you believe in God all of your life and He does exist, you have everything to gain. It is so evident that God does exist that there is no reason for me not to believe in Him. Faith in God helps enrich my soul. If I place all of my trust in God, I know that He will always provide for me and lead me toward what is right and what is just.

Dillon, 18

I feel God is the answer . . .

When I look around at everything in the world and nature, and see how awe inspiring it all is, I can't help but think that some greater force was at hand to produce all of it. I believe that force is God. I feel God is the answer and tailor of all the wonders of life. It is important to me to have this faith and belief in God because without it, life would feel very empty. He is something to look forward to after death and to help and inspire us during our time on Earth. The idea that there is an all-loving creator who conceived every human, every animal and every blade of grass with love and compassion makes me feel that I have a place and purpose in life. Even though there are the occasional doubts of faith, the times when I can actually feel God's presence overwhelm the doubts. If you believe in creation, love and friendship, then you believe in God, because He is all of these things and much more.

Salvador, 18

Once I discovered God, I learned . . .

I believe in God because He helped me to find myself. There was a point in my life when I had forgotten who I was. Everything around me was different. Kids at school were talking about me, and I started to believe everything that they were saying. It came to the point where I had to step out of my life, look at it, and change what was bad because when I looked at myself, I didn't like what I saw. My personality had become gray and colorless. My heart and my feelings were black and scarred. I was hurt and acting like someone I was not. I knew that I had to find something to grasp, to keep me strong and help me to find the real me. Finally, I found that something. It was a beautiful thing full of colors and everything good. For me, it was God. Once I discovered God, I learned that every time I have a problem or feel like I can't take it anymore,

God will be there. He helped make me strong. I was able to look at my life again and see everything in a different light. My attitude toward life and my friends was full of joy and happiness. The scars on my heart were still there, but for every scar, I was ten times smarter. God taught me that I can take my life and learn from everything. Slowly, He healed my heart. God turned my life around, and that is why I believe. If you are like I was, I hope that you can find God, too.

Keisha, 14

. . . we have to make faith our very own . . .

As long as I can remember, I went to church with my family on a regular basis and had a strong faith and commitment to the Lord. I was always brought up with good values and morals. I also had wonderful grandparents and great-grandparents with strong Christian values who set good examples for me, and I admire them. But as most teens know, we have to make faith our very own and not something we inherit from our parents. I had to make the decision for myself whether I wanted to accept God as my Lord and Savior. Two summers ago, I went to a Christian youth camp. I wasn't expecting anything to happen that didn't usually happen every Sunday when I went to church. I was very wrong, and it was then that I owned my faith and made the decision that I wanted God in my life, not just because I was expected to go to church every Sunday, but because I wanted Him to be a part of my everyday life. I met other teens, and I realized that it wasn't just me who had to face temptations and hardships, and that I wasn't alone.

I also discovered that when things like that do come up and someone isn't there to help me, I can just ask God, and He will give me the strength to face anything. Because no matter what, God accepts you for who you are and won't turn His back on you like a friend or boyfriend might. I have experienced miracles within my own family and have been blessed in feeling the comforting peace that God gives me when it seems no one else can. I have learned to trust the Lord with my future and live for Him daily. Whenever I have a problem, God is the first One I turn to. Under any circumstance, He is always there. He has filled my heart with joy.

Jaime, 15

I feel blessed . . .

I believe in God because He is always there whenever I have a problem. I know He will always be there guiding me toward the right path. I know that He hears me because when I am in doubt about something, I pray, and then I better understand what I should do. I feel blessed because God has been around me ever since I was born. My parents have always taught me to love God and trust and respect Him by their example. I have learned, by trusting God, He will show me what to do and help me on my journey through life, every little step of the way.

Jake, 15

*God doesn't care about
what kind of clothes you wear . . .*

*God: someone to trust, someone to believe in,
someone who believes in you. No matter what
religion you are or the way you believe in Him,
He's always there for you. You see, God doesn't
care about what kind of clothes you wear or who
your friends are. It doesn't matter to Him
whether or not you are in the "cool" crowd or
what you look like. He cares about you. He loves
you for who you are. No matter what kind of
day you've had, He's always there to listen,
always there to be your friend. So I am writing
this for you if you maybe aren't sure about God
and don't really know what to think. Maybe you
don't really know if you want to open your heart
to God or just don't know how. First of all, take
it slow. Start by talking to God and maybe read
some of the Bible. You don't have to go to church*

or be in a specific religion in order to believe or have trust in God. No matter what, know that He loves you. Just remember, when you have faith, you always have someone to turn to.

Brooke, 14

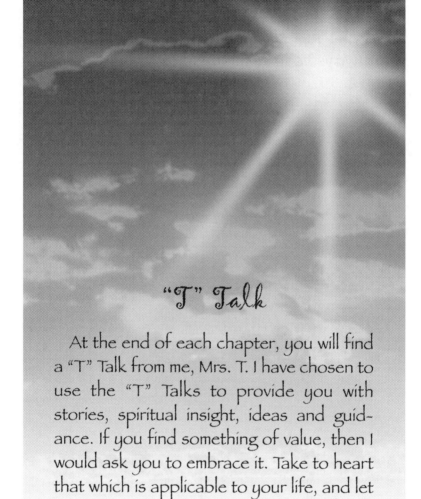

"T" Talk

At the end of each chapter, you will find a "T" Talk from me, Mrs. T. I have chosen to use the "T" Talks to provide you with stories, spiritual insight, ideas and guidance. If you find something of value, then I would ask you to embrace it. Take to heart that which is applicable to your life, and let it encourage and guide you as you grow in your faith.

CHAPTER TWO

Am I the Only One Who Doubts God?

"If you feed faith, doubt starves."

*I*f you have ever questioned the reality or presence of God, then the teen excerpts in this chapter may help you realize that you are not alone. However, I ask that you keep your heart open to the rest of the book, because I believe you will find a hope that is so often born in faith. If you identify with a passage written in this chapter, please keep reading, because as the saying goes: "If you feed faith, doubt starves." At the same time, if you don't identify with this chapter because you have never doubted God, then I encourage you to take these questions and doubts to heart, as they will help you to be more understanding while you grow in your faith.

Mrs. T

Where was God when I got dissed?

I'm having a really tough time in my life. Sometimes I feel lost and alone, and I can't find God. In one of those moments, I wrote this poem:

Where was God when I started to cry?
Where was God when I wanted to die?
Where was God when I felt left out?
Where was God when I screamed out?
Where was God when they judged me?
Where was God when no one would love me?
Where was God when I left my dad?
Where was God when I felt sad?
Where was God when I felt angry, violent and
   depressed?
Where was God when they made fun of the way
   I dress?
Where was God when she broke up with me?

*Where was God? He said He would always love
  me.*
Where was God when I got pissed?
Where was God when I got dissed?
Where was God when my hopes died?
The more I bend the harder they try.
Where was God when they put me down?
Where was God when they made me frown?
Where was God when I hated myself?
Where are you God? I need your help!

Thomas, 14

Have you ever wondered if God was there?

Have you ever wondered if God was there? I do it all the time. I do not know if He really exists. Look at all the wars, hunger and people who die unnecessarily. I know a lot of people ask these questions and doubt God. I do envy people who believe in God with no doubts or thought about it. I don't know if I could do it. Maybe the path to a perfect relationship or friendship with God is to have some doubts, just as we all usually doubt our friends about things they do, but we still trust them. The thing is, in order to do this, you have to have great faith, and that takes time. Maybe after some time and many trials and tribulations, I can believe that strongly. I am not saying that when I turn thirty I will have a great revelation, but it will take some time and I hope one day I will become a Christian with strong convictions.

Corbin, 17

*. . . we start questioning
if there is really a God . . .*

Being teenagers, we tend to rely on our friends for advice and guidance more than anyone else. Despite what parents or others say, teens more or less are prone to believe their friends' opinions more than elders or family members. Sometimes, when I talk to my friends about faith, we start questioning if there is really a God, and we do start to doubt our faith. This gets very confusing for me after listening to their conversations and then listening to my grandparents, for example. My family comes from a very religious background, and they encourage me to have faith in God. It is very frustrating, however, because I never know who to listen to: my family, who are wiser and more aware of what life has in store for people, or my friends, who are going through many of the same problems and stresses that I am. I want to stay in touch with God so that I can believe, but I still have doubts.

Kenya, 15

Sometimes, I wish that God would show me a sign . . .

Wherever I go, I hear about God. God this and God that. People say they believe in God because something happens to them or there was a sign. Sometimes, I wish that God would show me a sign so that I could believe. I've tried to believe, but as I've gotten older things have happened to me that cause me to still question if God is real. Also, I met some friends who have even worse problems than I have, so I ask, if there is a God, why would He let this happen to me and them? The more I think about it, the more I wonder. Why would God let people suffer so badly if He is so great? How do we know somebody didn't just make Him up? I hope someone didn't, though, because I really would like to believe.

Ronald, 15

Yet, I doubt Him . . .

Even though I am very blessed, I can't seem to find God in my life. Perhaps I am not searching for Him hard enough, or I am waiting for Him to come to me. I do not know. I have so much going on in my life. I don't feel like I can let anyone else in, even my protector and provider. I know the Lord is good to me, and I know He has given me incredible gifts. Yet, I doubt Him. I feel He will not be there to lead me to heaven. I fear He won't accept me. What if He doesn't understand me?

God, to me, is like a fact. Like, I know nature exists, and it contains great beauty and splendor, but I don't care. I know God is there, and He is doing so much for me, but I cannot directly see that; therefore, it doesn't matter. It is a harsh realization that I feel no connection with my God, but I don't know what to do. It is really a sad situation. I feel like I have plenty of time to find Him, and that He will always wait for me.

However, even worse, I myself am waiting for something. I am waiting for that great lightning bolt or the booming voice from the sky. Still, I think the chances of such things happening are very slim. So what am I doing, really? I am fooling myself. I am buying myself time and using my confusion as an excuse for my lacking efforts. I know these things. But I don't feel any impetus causing me to get on the road to change. I have seen God. I find Him every day. He is in my parents who sacrifice everything for my sister and me. He is in my dearest friends, who help me to see things differently and bring so much happiness to me. Most importantly, I find Him in the strangers, in the people who offer smiles for no reason and tell me to have a good day and really mean it. God is there. In fact, He is so close I could touch Him. However, these encounters with God are not enough. I cannot get true satisfaction from God's presence in others until I find Him in myself.

Jannessa, 18

Why does He let all the good kids die?

The concept of God confuses me. I just don't see how it is possible for a guy to make all of us little people. I have all of these questions: If there is a God, then who made Him? How can He know everything about everyone? How can He control every event that happens? Why does He let all the good kids die? But, on the other hand, how would all of us be here if not for God? I mean, everything has its maker. For instance, buildings don't just pop up without anyone making them, so isn't it the same with all of creation? Like our bodies—they're just perfect. We have everything we need, like eyes, ears, a nose and all of our organs. It's like someone designed us. So when I think that way, I think there must be a God. I still feel confused, though.

Billy, 14

. . . other times, I feel He is tired . . .

Have you ever felt confused about God? Well, I know I have. Sometimes I am a solid believer in Him and would debate anyone who said there is no God. But other times, I feel He is tired of the mistakes the world makes and turns away as if not to watch.

Daline, 14

. . . it is very hard for some people to believe in something they cannot see and touch . . .

Today, in a world of sin and betrayal, it is very hard for some people to believe in something they cannot see and touch. One of those people is me. I find it hard to believe in something if I have never totally witnessed it. Primarily, I think it is hard to find an honest and trustworthy person, let alone God. Finding an honest person today is like finding a diamond in the rough. Finding God, I think, is even more difficult. I have never seen or touched Him, and there is no scientific proof that He even exists. Although there are times when I feel I need Him, I am scared to pray to Him because I don't really have faith. I feel like a hypocrite if I pray and ask for His help. For me, faith in God is a very confusing thing. I have yet to really begin my *religious journey, and I am truthfully not in any hurry. However, I know there will be a time in my life that I will have to turn to God. I hope at that time that God will lead me through my confusion.*

Sarah, 17

. . . I am confused and doubtful . . .

Like Thomas in the biblical book of John, I am questioning my faith. I have gone through nine years of a private religious school, and during this time I have been told that God exists and that I do believe in Him. In all those years, I have never been asked if I actually do believe in God. Like Thomas, I would like to be shown that Jesus and God are real. Now that I have been asked, for the first time, what I believe in, I am confused and doubtful, and like many others I have questions that need to be answered. Will Jesus let me feel the wound in His side or give me another sign? Or will I have to discover faith on my own?

Mandie, 16

. . . God can't be scientifically proven . . .

I've had a little trouble during my life determining whether God is real. I say this because God can't be scientifically proven to be real. I try to find things in my life that I can credit to God, but I find it hard to believe that God would purposely kill or make innocent people suffer. At times, I feel that if there was a God, He wouldn't even be worth taking seriously because of what I consider to be His fickleness in His decisions. I haven't ruled out either way if He's real or not, so I am still trying to determine if He is worth following.

Carlos, 17

... I was convinced that God did not exist

There are many times in my life when I have felt confused about something. When confusion comes about in people's lives, they usually turn to God for guidance. However, how was I supposed to turn to God for help when He was what I was confused about? This question circled in my mind day after day. Is there really such a thing as God, or is He just a figment of our imagination?

Confusion is a very common thing in everyday life. Some get confused over friendships and relationships, and for others, parents and death are common issues of confusion. As a sophomore in high school, faith was what confused me. All of a sudden, the concept of God was escaping from my mind. And a new idea that there is no God was becoming a reality. I could not bring myself to go to church or even pray at all.

After both of my grandfathers died, three months apart, I was convinced that God did not exist. This way of life went on for about six months for me. In this span of six months, my faith had diminished into nothing.

However, as the year progressed, so did my faith. With the help of a few special friends and teachers, I left my ignorant state of mind while my faith in God and myself increased. I do not go to church as much as I should, but my faith in God is there in my heart. I find myself talking and praying to God whenever I can. My faith was made clear to me, and I learned many things about my religion that I have neglected in the past. As a result of this, I have become a new person physically and mentally. I am glad that I found my faith again, and I am glad that I believe in God.

Geffory, 18

... I lost faith in God.

Last year, confusion and sadness were daily issues in my life. My relationship with my best friend had fallen apart, and I honestly thought my world was over. Because of my lost friendship, I lost faith in God. I refused to go to church, and I couldn't stand it when people prayed in front of me. But then, over the summer, I met some new people, and my faith was renewed. I found out that my friendships with other people have a lot to do with my friendship with God. It wasn't God's fault that I had a falling-out with a friend. Maybe if I had listened to God, I would have recovered more quickly. He had better things waiting for me. I just didn't know it.

Heidi, 14

I used to think, "There is no God"

I believe in God. But sometimes, I used to get confused. Like sometimes I thought, "God is up in heaven just hanging out." And sometimes I thought, "There is no such thing as God." I began thinking that after my brother died about seven years ago. He had some kind of once-in-a-blue-moon cancer. I was only about six or seven, but I doubted that there was such a thing as God. About two years after that, my mom went to jail. I was depressed a lot. I used to think, "There is no God. If there was a God, He wouldn't let this all happen." But, I guess now I believe in God because I really don't have such a bad life. I mean, aside from all the usual bad stuff, my life is not all that bad. And I have come to see that what happens, happens. That's just life. If none of the bad stuff would have happened to me, I wouldn't be who I am today. So I guess, in a *way, I am glad God didn't change anything. I believe in God again, and I like who I am. Me.*

Reshaud, 14

I am confused about God . . .

I have been confused many times throughout my life. I entered ninth grade thinking it was going to be as easy as seventh and eighth grade. In the seventh and eighth grade your teachers baby you more, but when I got into ninth grade I felt like I was out on my own. There are so many more responsibilities. I had never spent an entire weekend just doing homework until ninth grade. My friendships also changed. I realized that the friends I grew up with weren't such good friends to me anymore, but I also made a lot of new friends. There have been weeks when my life is so hectic that I wonder if there is a God. There have been times that I pray for things to get better, yet they don't. Sometimes I feel like I should just run away, but then I realize how many people I would miss and who would miss me. God is so confusing! I don't go to church as much as I should, so I feel like I should be punished, or I think that God should make my week bad or something. Why didn't I feel this way when I was younger? I hated going to church, but now it is something I like to do. See how confused I am? I am confused about God, yet I want to go to church. I am confused about life right now. I don't even know how to fix it or where to begin to fix my problems. I pray that things will just get better, and sometimes they do. I just remember, or try to remember, that God never gives us more than we can handle.

Gina, 14

*. . . if there was no God,
then what was . . .*

When I was in the eighth grade, I began to doubt God. I was questioning everything I had always been taught. Like, that there was a God and that this God was all-loving and -forgiving. But all of a sudden, I was asking questions and I wasn't getting any answers. Also, at the time, my parents were fighting a lot and my older brother had just left for college, so I was feeling really alone. I prayed to God and asked Him to help my parents stop fighting and to give me all of the answers I needed. It didn't seem like God was even there. It just seemed like I was talking to nobody. None of my prayers were being answered, and my parents were getting worse. I was scared because if there was no God, then what was out there? Who was protecting us?

I started to not sleep. I just kept thinking about

there not being a God, and I was always freaking myself out. I would stay up as late as I could because I didn't want to think about it, and if I went to bed, it would consume my thoughts.

My mom finally asked me what was wrong, and I told her that I doubted there was a God because of all the stuff that our family was going through. I told her how I prayed for help and God never answered me. I told her about how I couldn't sleep at night because of it. So my mom started reading me this book about angels and all of these stories about people and how their guardian angel helped save their lives. She read to me until I fell asleep every night. By the time we finished the book, our family problems were starting to improve, I was getting my answers and I could finally sleep at night. I felt like I had betrayed God by doubting His existence, but I remembered what I had been taught. God is all-loving and -forgiving—and I have never doubted Him again.

Tobyn, 17

Does He think I think He's there . . .

When I was asked to write for this book, this poem flowed right from my heart to the paper. These are questions that I ask every day:

is He really there?
does He really hear my prayer?
does He ever sit and stare?
does He know my every thought?
does He know when I've been caught?
does He hear when I'm in doubt?
does He know when I shout?
does He know when I'm hurt?
does He know when I flirt?
does He think I think He's there?
does He really even care?
does He ever really know?
how can He ever show?
can He help me when I'm down?
can He save me when I frown?

does He really have the power
to sit and make the whole world cower?
is He able to make me share
all the things I wouldn't dare?
does He know when I am wrong?
does He know when I can't be strong?
does He ever stand right by
when I sit alone and cry?
is He really there for me
when no one else is there to see?
should I ever really believe
in something that I must conceive?
is there some way to show me how
He's really there, here and now?

Deena, 16

"J" Talk

There have been various times in my life when I have doubted God. I think that we all probably have. Perhaps you currently question the presence or reality of God. Maybe you believe in God but have experienced a situation in your life that caused you to mistrust God or your faith. I remember a time when I doubted the most. My memory takes me back to my freshman year of college when my mom called to tell me that my friend, Dana, had been killed in a car accident. I was overwhelmingly saddened over the loss of my friend, but even more than that, I was angry at God for the injustice of it all. After everything that Dana had been through, I didn't understand why a loving God would let this tragedy occur. You see, just a few years before, when Dana was sixteen and living in northern California with her dad, she was involved in her first car accident.

Dana's sunroof was open in her sporty little car as she slowed to a stop on the frontage road that met with her long driveway. As she waited to turn, the driver of a semi truck came barreling along the road behind her. By the time he realized that her car was stopped, it was too late. Upon collision, the impact was so extreme that Dana was ejected through the sunroof and thrown far into a field off the road. She landed with such force that, although there appeared to be no external injuries, she suffered from extensive internal trauma. Dana was in a coma for over six weeks, during which time her parents feared that she would die. As they prayed for her recovery, Dana fought deep inside her damaged body to live. Amazingly, she did.

The severity of Dana's brain injuries meant she had to learn the most basic tasks all over again. With determination, she started to talk, walk and regain control of her arms and hands. It was as if she was a mere toddler, taking baby steps. Each accomplishment was a praise to God. Several months after the accident, Dana moved in with her mom and stepdad. Although she continued to struggle with her speech and short-term memory, Dana finally felt that she had her life back. In fact, her best friend later told me that she thought Dana was perhaps more at peace than she had ever been.

Following her accident, Dana shared a wonderful relationship with her mom and stepdad. They were extremely close and came to appreciate each other in a way they hadn't before. Dana began going to church with her mom and accepted God into her life. She had graduated from high school and fell in love. Life looked bright! And now this. How could it happen to one person twice? I didn't understand. Why did she fight so hard to live, when she was going to die just a few short years later? Why would God take her, when He had given her such a wonderful second chance at life? None of it made sense to me. It occurred to me at the time that if God would let something like this happen, then I didn't know if I wanted to believe in Him. I questioned how He could even be real, because in my mind a real and loving God would not have caused her parents, fiancé and friends this much pain. He would not give them the hope of her life, only to snatch it away. For that matter, He wouldn't have given Dana the faith in a new start merely to deprive her of it before it even began. How could He?

Dana's mom was the one to answer that question for me. She explained that instead of feeling cheated, she felt blessed by God with the gift of three more years. For had Dana died after her first accident, they would not have had such quality time together these last few years. They had learned and loved so much. It was a time to treasure and be grateful for, she told me. I realized then that it was all about perspective. If Dana's mom could praise God during this time of tragedy, then why couldn't I? When I started to look at it from her point of view, I grew spiritually and personally. I came to realize that had I not doubted God, I would not have grown. The best part of my newfound insight, though, was that God understood my lack of faith.

Furthermore, I don't believe that doubting God hurts His feelings. Instead, I trust that it gives Him an opportunity to teach and love us. I understand how easy it is to jump into anger and frustration, put up a wall and turn your back on God. The sad part is that this doesn't benefit us in any way. Doubting God's presence and power is natural, but it is also lonely. When we allow ourselves to believe that God sees a bigger picture than we do, that His vision is incomprehensible to us, we might find acceptance in our doubt. We likely will not understand why we must experience sadness and loss, trial or tragedy, but we can find peace in our acceptance that God knows.

A friend of mine once used the analogy of a hole in a fence to help answer the questions of life situations that don't seem to make sense. She said that as people living in God's creation, it is like we are standing behind a fence. On the other side of the fence a parade is passing by. Unfortunately, the fence is tall, and we cannot see over it to glimpse a view of the parade. So we look through a little knot-hole that is present in a slat of the fence. We are able to see bits and pieces of the parade, but because our view is limited, we cannot conceive the entirety of the experience. This causes us to wonder why certain entries don't seem to match the theme or why a particular float is decorated in such a way. It is frustrating and confusing from our point of view. The colors don't flow, the bands are disconnected, we only see small portions of the floats, so it is difficult to tell what they represent. And most discouragingly, we don't know where the route leads. Yet from God's viewpoint, the parade is marvelous. He can see the complete procession, and therefore He fully understands the journey.

I often think of this comparison when I question

the purpose or outcome of certain situations in my life. Occasionally, I get frustrated when a person dies or experiences a hardship, and I hear someone else say, "Everything happens for a reason." For those of us who have felt the pain of losing a loved one or experiencing an injustice like hunger, neglect or abuse, there doesn't seem to be any "reason" on this Earth that is good enough. I have frequently felt that such a statement is extremely superficial. And yet, in a sense, this is where I now find hope. If we do not have the answers, then God does. Someday we will understand. However, in our present lack of understanding, we can grow, learn and accept God's love and comfort for us.

Keep in mind, faith is a journey. If you don't ask questions, then how can you learn and grow? You have to start somewhere. For you, like some of the teens who wrote for this chapter, that place might be outright disbelief. If so, that is okay. Yet I would hope that you will read this book with an open heart. For if you are open, then perhaps there will be something written on these pages that you can identify with. Maybe a teen will share an experience that is similar to something you have faced. Hopefully, through this book you will discover some answers to questions that have always confused you and create in you a desire to know more about God.

Also, know that if you do doubt God, your skepticism may have originated from an issue related to a specific religion. I pray that through this book you will find that turning to God does not have to be about religion; more importantly, it is about a relationship. I have spoken with many teens, as well as adults, who have been turned off by religion. Perhaps they have observed hypocrisy within a particular church, or maybe they don't agree with certain rituals. As such, religion can occasionally be the basis for disbelief. Please don't assume that I am saying religion is wrong, because I am not. Actually, religion can give us a foundation, structure and a community with which to enjoy fellowship. But religion without relationship can be meaningless. God calls you into a relationship with Him. When Jesus died and was resurrected, He sent the Holy Spirit so that you could have God with you always, so that you could know God, feel Him and have a relationship with Him. Qualities of a healthy relationship include conversation, understanding, loyalty and love. The Bible promises that God is committed to this type of relationship and desires it with you.

On the other hand, if you have already accepted the Lord into your life, then you know how wonderful and fulfilling a relationship with Him can be. Frequently, people who consider themselves believers feel guilty if or when they doubt God. If you have ever felt this way, please know that God understands it when we question Him. He doesn't condemn us for our doubt. A Christian leader once told me that he believed that God actually liked us to doubt. He said, "Without doubt, we sometimes get stagnant in our relationship with God. Yet when we ask questions of God, we become energized to find the answers." And even if you don't find the answers that you may be looking for, as many teens shared in this chapter, God will still be waiting for you when you are ready to turn to Him. He is also prepared to guide you from your disbelief and help you rediscover your faith.

Despite your current spiritual beliefs, there is a reason that we doubt. Doubt causes us to question. As we question, we discover; as we discover, we grow. It is likely that our life journeys are going to take us down different roads. But if we welcome growth upon our path through life, it will enrich our hearts and fill us with hope. As you read through the pages of this book, I pray that you open the door to your heart and allow your faith to begin to grow.

CHAPTER THREE

God, Grant Me Courage

. . . if you read a passage that you have difficulty identifying with . . .

We all encounter situations in our lives in which we experience a need for courage. Our reasons may be extremely simple or quite complex. Some of the teens who wrote for this chapter share serious problems that led to their prayer for courage. Others express a need for boldness that stems merely from ordinary teen angst. Despite the reasons, I hope that the passages you are about to read will lead you to think about the many ways the Lord provides us with courage and strength. I also pray that if you read a passage that you have difficulty identifying with because of a sensitive topic such as suicide or addiction, you will use that excerpt to help you understand what a fellow student or a close friend may be experiencing. Let these stories give you insight and understanding. Perhaps, even, let them give you the courage to reach out and help someone in need.

Mrs. T

I worried about every possible thing that could go wrong . . .

I used to think courage was a gift given only to a select few; a person either had it or she didn't. I think many people, especially teens, feel the same way. The last place most people would look for courage would be in God, but I found courage, as well as strength, in God. When I was young, I truly believe I was fearless; I could remember not being afraid of anything. I wasn't scared to try new things, to go against the norm, or to be the person I was inside.

I am not sure exactly when that all changed, but I think it was around the time I entered high school. For the first time in my life, I was nervous on the first day of school. I wasn't a nervous type of person; in fact, I rarely got nervous, but that day I was so nervous I almost felt sick. It seemed odd to me to get so worked up about something *as silly as school, but I couldn't help myself. I worried about every possible thing that could go wrong; at the time, I didn't think I had ever been so scared in my life. On the way to school that morning, I looked to God. I felt that He was the only one who could make me feel any better. I didn't ask God to take away my nervousness or to make everything go perfectly on my first day of high school. I simply asked Him to be with me because I felt that I needed Him. I walked into school that morning, and I felt that God was with me. He filled me with courage. My nervousness didn't disappear, but it was eased and that was all I needed.*

Holli, 18

. . . I only could call on my Lord . . .

I know that sometimes when I talk with God, it is only to ask for help and never to say a simple, "Thanks, God." But God is always there, and I know that because He helped me in the most terrifying moment of my life. I am seventeen years old; that situation happened three years ago. I am from another country, and that happened in my country. I was walking to my home at 4:30 P.M., and I felt that something or some person was following me. My hair stood on end. I stopped walking. I turned around and, in that moment, my heart stopped for a second. I saw three young teens, two on bicycles in front of me, one with a small knife behind me. "What?" I asked, my hands shaking without control. "You have a trade, smart guy: your life or your money," answered the tallest of the group. With no money in my pockets, my heart pushing my

*chest trying to explode, I only could call on my
Lord, God. Ten seconds later, a strange man
whom I had never seen before started to call me.
The strange man made the other guys run. I
never saw that man again, but I am sure that
God is courage because he shared it with me that
day and sent a stranger to save my life.*

Shay, 18

. . . even in my loneliest hour, I have never felt alone

Mark Twain once said, "Be good, and you will be lonely." Now what he didn't say is that being lonely is not the same as being alone. You see, throughout my life, I have always tried to be honest and do the right thing, even if it wasn't the most popular choice. Hence, some of these choices have thrown me into a state of loneliness. However, even in my loneliest hour, I have never felt alone. There has always been a light in the darkness, a voice in the silence, an existence in the void. God has always been my sentinel, watching over and protecting me when I truly needed a guardian. God has also given me the courage and the strength to pull myself out of these states of loneliness. Unlike Icarus, from Greek mythology, who had no one to catch him when he fell from the heavens, I feel that God is *always by my side, ready to fix my wings and allow me to fly again.*

James, 17

It was like this phenomenal sense of courage enlightened me . . .

About two years ago, my grandpa was, to put it bluntly, on his deathbed dying of cancer. He couldn't speak clearly; he kept talking gibberish, mostly. It was really a hard time for everyone, including me. I hadn't been that close to my grandfather—he was always in the back of his house in his room, away from the cheerful family gatherings. See, he was a big alcoholic back then. Maybe all that bitter wine made him bitter. I even think that maybe that's how he got the cancer. I guess I wasn't as sad as I could or should have been since, like I said, we weren't too close.

When I got up enough courage to go in the depressing room, I just started to break down and cry like crazy. I don't know what came over me. I just couldn't stop the tears from flowing. I *just couldn't do it; I guess I didn't have the courage after all. What was even weirder was what happened next. My mom sat me down in the next room and began to try to comfort me. The next thing I knew, my tears were gone and I was filled with this amazing confidence, almost instantly. It was like this phenomenal sense of courage enlightened me in a matter of seconds. I feel it was God who helped me through it, because after that I walked back into my grandfather's room, held his hand and talked to him— without even trembling. My mother's words had comforted me, but I feel something more than that made me feel so safe and all right. I wasn't a strong, daily believer of God then, but now I know that He does things in our lives for a purpose, and I thank Him every day for that.*

Lanya, 15

. . . all my friends turned against me

Years ago, and even recently, I have felt alone. I felt like no one in the world was there for me to lean on. I have even sometimes thought of ending my pain. I remember a specific time when I was sitting upstairs alone in my room. My boyfriend and I had just broken up. To make matters worse, all my friends turned against me. I remember the tears streaming down my face, and it seemed like they would never end. I yelled up to God, asking how He could let me lose everything I held dear. I was so angry that He let me feel so alone that I felt taking my life was the only way out. Then, out of nowhere, I started praying. I said the prayer without even realizing it. I asked God for his forgiveness. Suddenly, my tears stopped. Instead of screaming at God, I was thanking Him. In doing this, I remembered something that someone had once told me: "You are never alone because God is always there." To me, knowing that God is always there spiritually and that He is never going to abandon me is the greatest knowledge I have gained. Although I know that He did not physically wipe the tears off my face that night, He did help the tears to cease. He gave me the strength to appreciate my life. Since that night, I have put my total faith, love and trust in God and understand that everything happens for a reason. I believe that God gave me the courage to know that everything will eventually turn out for the best.

Kandace, 15

AUTHOR'S NOTE: *Kandace suggests that when everything in her life was going wrong, she thought of ending her life. Please recognize that instead of turning to suicide, Kandace turned to God. Taking one's life is not the answer and definitely not God's desire for you. If you have ever contemplated suicide, please seek comfort and courage from God and find the strength in Him to talk to someone about what you are feeling or to call the National Suicide Hotline at 1-800-SUICIDE (1-800-784-2433). Also, please take time right now to refer to the "T" Talk at the end of this chapter for reassurance and guidance.*

. . . I thought fitting in would be the most important thing in my life . . .

When I was younger, the realization that I was fat came from other people's hurtful words and mean comments. I would always try to hide from people and their words. I would cry so much, and my tears would sting my cheeks with shame for myself and what I looked like. Because I thought fitting in would be the most important thing in my life, it just made me even more excluded. I kept to myself, and I avoided people. Yet, they came and found me, just to put me down and make fun of the way I looked. I was always in tears, but no one saw them. No one saw the pain I was really feeling because I hid behind a plastic smile and fake laugh. I was lost and confused and didn't know where to go. Whenever I went out to recess, they would make a game out of hurting my feelings or making me cry. I was always in tears, and my friends weren't even there when I needed them the most. They would say that they felt sorry for me but were too afraid it would hurt their own image if they stuck up for me. I had no one, and I was too alone to be human. I felt one-of-a-kind and hated it. Then I went to a youth group and my eyes were opened because I saw Christ. He opened not just my eyes, but also my heart and gave me the courage to love myself for who I was and not what I looked like. I asked Him to lift my problems off my shoulders. He helped me through everything. He showed me that it is great to be one-of-a-kind and that is exactly what I am.

Maddison, 13

READER/CUSTOMER CARE SURVEY

675705862

We care about your opinions. Please take a moment to fill out this Reader Survey card and mail it back to us.
As a special **"thank you"** we'll send you exciting news about interesting books and a valuable **Gift Certificate**

Please PRINT using ALL CAPITALS

Name
First _____ MI. □ _____
Last
Name _____

Address _____

City _____ ST □ Zip _____

Phone # (□□□) □□□ - □□□□ Fax # (□□□) □□□ - □□□□

Email _____

BA1

(1) Gender:
○ Female
○ Male

(2) Age:
○ 13-19   ○ 40-49
○ 20-29   ○ 50-59
○ 30-39   ○ 60+

(3) Your children's age(s):
Please fill in all that apply.
○ 6 or Under   ○ 15-18
○ 7-10   ○ 19+
○ 11-14   ○ 1   ○ 3
               ○ 2   ○ 4+

(8) Marital Status:
○ Married
○ Single
○ Divorced / Widowed

(9) Was this book:
○ Purchased For Yourself?
○ Received As a Gift?

(10) How many HCI books have you bought or read?
○ 1   ○ 3
○ 2   ○ 4+

(11) Did this book meet your expectations?
○ Yes
○ No

(12) How did you find out about this book? *Please fill in ONE.*
○ Personal Recommendation
○ Store Display
○ TV/Radio Program
○ Bestseller List
○ Website
○ Advertisement/Article or Book
○ Catalog or Mailing
○ Other _____

(13) What FIVE subject areas do you enjoy reading about most? *Choose 1 for your favorite, 2 for second favorite, etc.*

	1	2	3	4	5
Self Development	○	○	○	○	○
Parenting	○	○	○	○	○
Spirituality/Inspiration	○	○	○	○	○
Family and Relationships	○	○	○	○	○
Health and Nutrition	○	○	○	○	○
Recovery	○	○	○	○	○
Business/Professional	○	○	○	○	○
Entertainment	○	○	○	○	○
Sports	○	○	○	○	○
Teen Issues	○	○	○	○	○
Pets	○	○	○	○	○

FOLD HERE

BA1

9396058864

(18) Where do you purchase most of your books?
Please fill in your top TWO choices only.

- ○ General Bookstore
- ○ Religious Bookstore
- ○ Warehouse / Price Club
- ○ Discount or Other Retail Store
- ○ Website
- ○ Book Club / Mail Order

(20) What type(s) of magazines do you SUBSCRIBE to?
Fill in up to FIVE categories.

- ○ Parenting
- ○ Sports
- ○ Fashion
- ○ Business / Professional
- ○ World News / Current Events
- ○ General Entertainment
- ○ Homemaking, Cooking, Crafts
- ○ Women's Issues
- ○ Other (please specify) _____

(25) Are you:
- ○ A Parent?
- ○ A Grandparent

Was I really being left alone?

Growing up, my life was okay. We had some tough times, but we always knew we would get through it as a family. I lived with my dad and my brother, and I always knew we would be all right. But when I was thirteen, our family started falling apart. I'm not sure how it all came about, but little things created heated arguments. My dad and older brother were constantly crashing into each other in an endless battle of who was right.

One night stands out the most to me because I discovered a faith that was stronger than the anger. My dad and brother were fighting (nothing new), but this time was far worse. I was brought into it. I felt harsh words lash out at me from my father with cold cruelness. At that point, I would have rather experienced physical pain than hear what he had just said to me. My dad, full of rage and fury, put on his jacket and took off. My brother, in the same state of mind, was packing his stuff preparing to run away. I felt my world caving in around me. Was I really being left alone? I didn't want the fights, but I didn't want to be alone either. My brother left the room, and at that moment I felt completely hopeless. I hit the ground with angry tears streaming down my face and begged God to help me. I asked Him to give me the courage it would take to be the one to hold it together. I asked Him to give them both forgiveness for each other. In that instant, I felt about a thousand times lighter. Then my tears of frustration turned into those of determination. I got up and went out to find my dad. I made both my dad and brother come back to the house. I made them talk and, more importantly, I encouraged them to listen. For once in my life, they heard what I said.

Since then, things are getting better. A lot of time has passed, and it hardly ever gets that bad. I know God was with me that night, and I know He gave me the courage to reach the unreachable. I am not perfect when it comes to religion, but I am a believer. I know God was with me that night, and I know He will always be with me when I need Him. I have put my trust in God's hands. I know that with Him, I will be safe. It doesn't matter what this life brings; God will see me through it. I know great things are waiting for me. All I need to do is stay with God.

Gabriella, 15

She has herself and her family fooled . . .

I'm worried about a friend of mine. Maybe you have a friend like this, too. I put my thoughts down in this poem:

I have this friend, we've been friends forever
But now our friendship doesn't seem to measure
She's lost so much weight in this past year
If she doesn't seek help, the end will be near
She has herself and her family fooled
Her obsession with being skinny has overruled
When I try to talk
She gets mad and walks
Although I know deep inside
She isn't mad, she is just trying to hide
She's quit the sports she's loved and been
   good at
Because now her body won't let her do that

I have thought and thought of what to do
My other friends feel it is their fault, too
My friends and I have done everything we
    possibly could
I hope she'll turn to God for courage, like
    she should
There is nothing left for me to do
But to know that God will help her through

Nina, 14

AUTHOR'S NOTE: Eating disorders are extremely danger-
ous and need to be taken seriously, as they can threaten
one's health and life. If you currently are struggling with an
eating disorder, please allow yourself to reach out for help.
Talk to your parents, pastor, friend or an adult whom you
trust. You may also find it helpful to contact Eating Disorders
Awareness and Prevention (EDAP), an eating-disorder
information and referral hotline, at 1-800-931-2237.

I thanked God for giving me this peace in my heart . . .

In the past six months, I have really gotten a lot of courage and strength from the Lord. I come from a very extensive Native American family, and we all love each other with our hearts and souls. In the past six months, I have lost five loved ones, and this hurt me badly. It has been two months since the last death. I was close to all of them, especially my great-grandma. We shared the same soul. Although I felt angry that my loved ones were gone, I still found strength in the Lord.

About three days after my great-grandmother's death, I had an experience that can't be explained. I was feeling terrible, and I couldn't eat or get out of bed. I was dozing off to sleep when I heard three knocks on my bedroom window. I was frightened. I sat up on my bed and leaned against the wall. I saw a light. It wasn't very bright, but it was glowing. I heard two women laughing, and they sounded very happy. Not only did they sound happy, they sounded like my beautiful great-grandma and my little auntie. She was my great-grandma's sister who passed away only three months before. I was no longer scared. I felt warm inside. I fell to sleep never saying a word or trying to speak to them, just listening to their sweet voices that used to whisper me to sleep. I woke up feeling peace, remembering the last time I saw my great-grandma. She told me, "Don't stay away too long," and I said, "You either." She said, "You better come visit me." I said, "You, too." And that's exactly what she did! I thanked God for giving me this peace in my heart, for I did not get to say good-bye before her death. Also, I thanked God for giving me the courage to accept my great-grandmother's death and go on with my life.

Luci, 14

I was scared . . .

I was always confused when I was little. When I look back at how my life was, I don't think it was a very good one. Of course, I always had fun playing with my friend on the swings and stuff, but when it came to what went on at home, I didn't like it. My mom was always having new people over, people I had never even seen before. I thought they were going to be some new friends or something. I was a little confused about it, but I never asked because of what I can remember about my mom. She always seemed to be in a bad mood or not wanting to be around me at all.

One day, my mom did not come home at night. My dad got out of work at 5:00. I was supposed to be picked up from school at 3:00. I had to sit at the school for two hours, and finally the cops had to come and pick me up. I was scared out of my mind. When I got home my dad was just *showing up. I was happy to be home, but scared and confused because I didn't know what was going on. That night I found out that my mom was in jail for drugs. I was also confused about what drugs were. I learned that the people who always came to my house were people who were dealing drugs with my mom.*

Eventually, my dad left my mom, and we moved and started over. I remember my new next-door neighbor came over to meet me and I started talking to her. She had a lot of belief in God. I used to think that maybe there was no God, because I didn't think He was ever there to help me. My new neighbor showed me that God was there. She said that maybe I experienced everything with my mom for some reason that I wouldn't understand until I was older. She also looked me in my eyes and said, "Nita, God does have faith in you to go to school, get good grades and stand up for yourself. He will give you the courage you need." So I figured I would try to believe in myself. If God believes in me, maybe I could, too. And He did give me courage. Even with all my family problems, I do excellently in school, and I have a lot of new friends. Mostly, because I now have a really strong belief in God.

Nita, 14

AUTHOR'S NOTE: *Sadly, some teens come from homes in which a parent is addicted to drugs or alcohol. If you or someone you know is living with an addict and needs help or support, I encourage you to contact your local chapter of Al-Anon, Alateen or a similar program that provides support for families living with addicts. You can call 1-888-4-AL-ANON (1-888-425-2666) to find an organization near you.*

"J" Talk

Joe was one of my best friends in high school. He was the type of guy whom everyone loved. He had a strong faith in the Lord, but at that time in his life, he lived for his friends. Although he was an outstanding athlete, he was able to supersede the typical high school cliques. He was full of life and always ready for a fun time. One of the things that I enjoyed most about Joe was the delight he took in luring someone into a good prank. Maybe I enjoyed it so much because he and I pulled many pranks on one another. One of Joe's favorite schemes, which he carried out with another close friend of ours, was to sneak into my locker, take the keys to my truck and then move it to various places around our school. When I would go out to the parking lot after school, I'd never quite know where I'd find my truck. Once it was on the other side of the football field. Another time, it was behind the convenience store across the street. I never figured out how they pulled it off without getting into trouble, especially when they left it for me to find on our school's front lawn. The ultimate fun, however, was worth their efforts. It seems ironic now that while my truck was the source of so much amusement for us, Joe's truck carried him into the greatest tragedy of his life.

It was a typical Friday night in a small town. Joe and his friend, Ronnie, were on their way to a party. It was dark out, and he and Ronnie were listening to the radio, cruising along. All of a sudden, Ronnie screamed, "Joe . . . STOP!" Within an instant, Joe felt a sickening thud and watched his right wind-shield shatter into pieces. Joe never saw the man who had wandered into the road, but the second he felt the impact, he knew that he had just hit a human being. Can you imagine what went through his mind? Joe told me later that everything inside him wanted to run. He said that his first thoughts were, "Just keep driving," as if ignoring this terrible calamity might make it go away. But he knew that his conscience would not allow that to happen. So Joe pulled to the side of the road. As he got out of his truck, he looked back to see a limp, mangled body. Ronnie raced to call for an ambulance, while Joe ran over to where the man lay lifeless in the middle of the road. He felt so helpless as he approached, because as he encountered the man's crumpled body, he knew inside that the man was already dead.

While Joe waited for the police and ambulance to arrive, his own life flashed before his eyes. Questions filled his mind. How could this have happened? How could he have killed someone? How could his life change so fast? One moment Joe was on his way to laugh, joke and live it up with friends at a party, and in the next instant he was kneeling over a man, willing him to breathe. It didn't seem fair. He wasn't driving recklessly, drinking or even speeding. The road was clear, and then out of nowhere there was this man.

As these thoughts swirled around in Joe's mind, he subtly began to feel a very small sense of peace. He couldn't explain this feeling except to say that it could only have come from God, for the

circumstances that he had found himself in were too
overwhelming to even comprehend. As statements
were taken, Joe learned that the man he hit was
homeless and had been walking along the road with
another man. The man told the police that he had
told his friend not to walk in the road. But the victim
had been drinking and had lost his sense of good
judgment. He had no identification, no family and no
home. While Joe was taken to have his blood tested
to confirm that he had not been drinking, the man
was taken to the morgue. All the while, Joe's heart
was pounding with the reality of the accident. Yet,
he knew that he had to focus on the sense of peace
that he was feeling, because without it, Joe knew
that fear would overwhelm him.

Mostly, Joe feared that all of his dreams and
desires for the future would vanish as quickly as this
horrifying accident that had just transpired. He
feared that he would lose control of his life and his
destiny. You see, Joe had always wanted to be a
cop. It had been his goal for as long as he could
remember. Would he never realize this dream? Or
worse, would he end up on the other side of it,
behind bars? Joe also feared the reaction of his
family and friends. What would they think, and what
would they say? Throughout the days following the
accident, Joe contemplated all of these things and

knew that he had an important decision to make. He could give up and hide behind his fears, or he could seek the courage he would need to face the repercussions of this tragic ordeal.

Joe chose to grasp on to that underlying peace that had been steadfast throughout his fear and confusion. Daily, Joe put his situation in God's hands, and that sense of peace nurtured a feeling of courage that he knew he would not have experienced on his own. Joe knows that without God's touch, he could have withered away. But with God, he was able to hold his head up, face his fears and grow emotionally, as well as spiritually.

I, on the other hand, struggled with my role as Joe's friend. How do you support someone who has experienced something so tragic? As a sixteen-year-old, I was scared. On the day following the accident, I picked up the phone to call Joe fifteen different times, but hung it up before I dialed because I was afraid that I would say the wrong thing. When I finally did make the call, I was relieved when Joe's mom told me that he wasn't up to talking. I comforted myself with, "At least you tried." I could have done so much more, but I just didn't have the courage. I remember praying for Joe, but not praying for myself to find the courage to be the friend that Joe needed me to be in his time of need.

I understand now that the courage we tend to lack as teens can be found in the strength and power of God. Had I asked God to give me the courage to comfort my friend, I believe I would have had the confidence to show up on his front doorstep, if only to say, "I'm here for you." But, I was afraid, so I made excuses. As teenagers, it is easy to make up a reason for not taking action by convincing ourselves that it is for the better. When really, we may just not have the courage that it takes to do the right thing. I told myself that Joe needed his space, that he didn't want to see anyone and needed time with his family. It took me almost a week to work up the courage on my own to get over to Joe's house and be there for him as a friend. Yet, in the Bible, Jesus says, "Ask and it shall be given unto you, seek and you shall find." Courage is waiting in that scripture. As I look back, I wish that I would have sought such strength from God.

If you have struggled with an experience in your life where you have needed the courage to endure, look to God. When someone dies, for example, it seems so senseless to us, so unfair. We get lost in our grief, and that is a very lonely place to be. Sometimes we even turn our backs on God. But, turning toward God instead of away from Him can bring understanding, peace and even hope to your heart.

Maybe your need for courage is more serious. Perhaps you need it because you question the value of your life. If, like Kandace, you have ever considered suicide, please know that taking your own life is not the answer to your hopelessness. I have heard teens occasionally express that they feel it takes courage to commit suicide. I disagree. I believe that it takes courage to live. Think about this: If your life is so bad that you consider suicide as your only option, then it *has* to get better. And, if it is going to get better, why would you want to die?

I have spoken to numerous teens who have admitted to thinking about suicide. So know that if you have ever considered it, you are not alone. Yet that doesn't mean that attempting suicide, let alone completing a suicide, is right. One of my former students, Anthony, told me that when he gets in the mind-set of having nothing left to live for, he turns it around and considers that if, in fact, that is the case, then he has nothing left to lose. This keeps him focused on living rather than dying. Another student, Summer, once shared that she saw her life as an endless book. Each page was a new day. She said that if teens get to the point where they are considering suicide, then all they needed to do was wait until the next day, because it was a whole new page, and who knows what excitement or happiness could be waiting there. Just like a book, our life stories change. If we take it upon ourselves to end our lives, we miss out on the story in its entirety, and the story could have an incredibly happy ending.

In addition, when contemplating suicide, teens frequently neglect to think about the people they would hurt by their choice. They tend to disregard the consequences of fatal actions. Do you think that God, who loves you so much, who in essence created you and gave you life, would want you to take your life into your own hands? Have you ever asked yourself if suicide isn't, in reality, murder? Now, I'd be willing to bet that you would never think about killing another person, so why would you kill yourself? In God's eyes, perhaps it is the same. What do you think?

Regardless of your answer, know that God has a gift waiting for you. It is not wrapped in beautiful paper with a perfect bow. In fact, He has already opened it and placed it in a small room in your heart. It is courage, and it is waiting there to be discovered by you. When you do find it, if you keep your eyes focused on God as you approach, the courage He has placed in your heart will blossom into the strength that you need to see you through your most difficult trial or turbulent time. Like my friend

Joe, if you put your life in God's hands daily, He will give you the courage that you need to persevere.

AUTHOR'S NOTE: *If needed, please take time to turn to Appendix II at the end of the book for additional referral services for grief and loss, suicide, drug addiction, eating disorders and more.*

CHAPTER FOUR

You Are My Strength!

. . . the Lord will provide you with courage and strength . . .

Some of the excerpts written in this chapter deal with very serious issues. Teens write of experiences such as drug use, abuse and grief. Although I understand that these topics are quite extreme, I have chosen to include them in this chapter in order to demonstrate that even in the most desperate of situations, the Lord will provide you with courage and strength to endure such life experiences. I realize that you may read this chapter and think, "Gosh, my life experience is mild compared to some of these people. Why would God take time for my little problems?" God does take time because He loves you. If you need the strength to deal with the pressures of achieving academically or meeting your parents' expectations, God will provide. Or perhaps you've prayed for the courage to reach out and make a new friend. God knows the importance of your prayer. You don't need to be dealing with a severe situation in order to call out to God for courage or strength. On the other hand, if you do identify with some of the serious issues addressed in this chapter, feel free to turn to the "T" Talk at the end of the chapter for reassurance and advice. Also, pray for the courage to talk to a trusted adult. Regardless, please know that whatever your situation, mild or extreme, God will be there.

Mrs. T

*I don't have the courage
or the strength in me
to stand up and say no . . .*

I will be the first one to admit that I don't have a strong personality. Peer pressure is a hard thing for me to deal with because of that. I don't have the courage or the strength in me to stand up and say no. Sometimes I end up doing stupid things, and people get upset with me, but no matter what, God is always there. In some situations, I find it easy to just step back, reflect, weigh the consequences and let God guide me to the right decision. I know that He can provide me with the strength to say no if I honestly don't want to regret a potential poor choice because of peer pressure. So when I don't have the strength to say no, I look to God and use His strength.

Brianna, 15

I returned from my vacation uncertain of where we were to live and how we were going to survive . . .

"You are a strong person" were the only comforting words I received from my father when he told me there had been a fire and we had lost everything. I had been camping with a friend during one of the hottest weeks of July 1999 when a fire spread across the six-family apartment where I lived, leaving nothing to spare. I returned from my vacation uncertain of where we were to live and how we were going to survive. During this time of finding a place to live and buying new belongings through donated money, I began to feel very frustrated with God. My head was filled with questions. Why me? Why did my home have to burn down? Why did my parents have to be divorced? Why couldn't I have a normal life? Eventually, I realized I had no right to be frustrated with God; in fact, I should be thankful that He had given me these experiences. God had allowed these things to happen to me not because He wanted to see me suffer, but because He knew I could handle them. I began to see that through my trials, God's strength led me to become a stronger person, and through my experiences I have been able to help others in need of guidance through their hard times.

Randee, 18

In my heart I knew
what I had to do . . .

My senior year of high school was definitely an experience . . . full of fun and friends, but also trials. When finals rolled around, my brain was not the only thing being tested; my heart and my conscience were as well. About a week before the scheduled final for one of my hardest classes, a rumor began circulating that three guys in my class were going to steal our teacher's final. Very quickly the bidding began. It felt like the entire class was offering to pay the guys as long as they got a copy of the final ahead of time. Right away, I was posed with three differ-ent choices.

My first option was to take advantage of this amazing opportunity. I mean, not every day a final is available ahead of time, and I had so many to study for. I was nervous about all of my upcoming finals; having this one taken care of would definitely lighten my study load. I would only have to come up with the proper sum of money, deliver it to those gutsy guys, and I'd have it made: one A+ in the bag, baby!

My second option was slightly different, but at least it would save me money. I could not participate in this very risky and very illegal endeavor. I'd just ignore what it felt like everyone was doing, study for the final and most definitely sulk as I saw my classmates receive their A+s.

The last option was by far the most difficult. Up until this time, what I did affected no one; if I joined them they'd be happy (at least about the extra money), and if I stood by and minded my own business they wouldn't care. My problem was that little cricket sitting on my shoulder screaming in my ear.

The voice of the cricket was, of course, God. In my heart I knew what I had to do. I had to tell my teacher what was going on; he had to know the plot to steal the final. Doing this would surely provide me with a long list of brand-new enemies all foaming at the mouth ready to kill me for spoiling their A+s. The strength to go to my teacher, knowing full well how many people would hate me after I did, was not my own but the Lord our Father's.

The afternoon I chose to divulge my information felt like an eternity. As I walked up the seemingly endless steps to my teacher's office, a voice in my head kept repeating to me: *Your rewards will not come in this life, but in heaven.* That voice was the only thing that made me climb those steps. All the way up, there was a screaming match going on inside my head, because there was also a voice crying out that I was flushing a perfectly good A+ down the toilet. Anyway, I made it up the steps and was somehow able to muster the courage to knock on my teacher's door and actually take a seat across from him at his desk. I told him the truth, the whole truth and nothing but the truth (so helped by God, of course), and I actually survived. Many times I told myself I could not face the situation, for it was just too difficult. I did somehow, and the relief I felt after the fact was wonderful.

If left to my own human weakness, I have no doubt I would have given in, forked over the dough and taken, actually stolen, the A+. Instead, because of the strength from God, I know I did the right thing; I can look at myself *in the mirror every morning with no shame and actually a bit of pride. I took the test, which my teacher undoubtedly made a great deal harder after I left his office, and got a B. My grades are very important to me, but I treasured this B, not for its value in my GPA, but for what it said. The strength I lacked to do the right thing was made up for by God, and that B will forever remind me!*

Mariah, 19

Sometimes I just don't know what to do or say . . .

Many times life throws us a pitch that we don't see coming. Life, and sometimes even God, get confusing. You know the types of things I am talking about: a divorce in the family, a friend or a friend's parent dying, or the loss of any loved one, for that matter. Sometimes I just don't know what to do or say in situations like this. Cancer has seemed lately like it is taking over the world. I swear I must know at least eight people with cancer and two who have died from it. It seems so unreal sometimes, and it's hard to swallow the fact that a living human I saw days before is in a casket with his or her family weeping over them. These are times when I am confused, and I need God's strength and guidance. It feels like nobody can comfort me sometimes, so I talk to God about things. I don't usually use *specific prayers; I just have a personal conversation with God. No matter how hard times get, they always seem to get better. People say time is a healer, but they are mistaken. God is the one taking their burdens away. Sometimes I wish people would realize this, but I know eventually things will come together and work out.*

Andrew, 17

That's when I got into drugs . . .

In the beginning of the sixth grade, my parents were starting to have some big problems. Each time they fought, the yelling and fighting seemed to get worse. About the middle of that year, my parents got a divorce. That devastated me. I have always relied on my family. Now my family was all broken apart. My little brothers and sisters were too young to understand, my mom didn't seem to care, and my dad was moving to another state. My life was falling apart. I started hanging out with some older friends all the way through that year. I noticed they were into drugs, parties, girls and alcohol. But I didn't do that stuff because my mom and I were very close and I didn't want to do that to her.

Well, about the summer before my seventh-grade year, my mom started seeing this guy. He was nice, very religious, and he treated my mom like gold. I was happy for her at first, but then she started to get serious with him. She started spending all of her time with him and not much time with me. That's when I got into drugs. I started to hang out with those friends a lot more. All we did was drink, do drugs, go to parties, sneak out and get into trouble.

My mom noticed the change in me. I was never home, I would talk back, my grades slipped badly, I hated her boyfriend and I never did what she asked. I know she suspected that I was using, but she had no proof. Still, I was excluding myself from my good friends, my family and my real self. My mom got worried, and she and her boyfriend sat me down and talked to me. They asked me if I was using drugs and all that stuff. I denied it all. I just told them what they wanted to hear.

We all got up, but then my mom's boyfriend pulled me to the side and asked me if I knew God. I said, "Of course I know God, I've gone to church and I know He is there." He said, "No, do you actually know God?" I was like, "No I don't know Him." He told me a lot about God that night. He told me that I needed to open my eyes and realize that there is something greater than me, and then he asked me how my life was going. I said, "Good, I guess" but I knew that inside my life was in pieces. And I know he saw right through me. He said, "God is there. He will listen and He will answer. He will be your strength." He also said, "If you don't believe me, just try to discover God yourself, but mean it." He challenged me that night to read the book of John from the New Testament. I did and just reading that one book changed a lot of my thinking. I realized that there is someone greater than me, who has a never ending love for me and gave His Son for me. I sat in my bed that night, and I wept while asking God to forgive me for all that I had done and all who I had hurt. I asked Him to help me in my ways, give me the strength to resist my temptations and be with me.

As I began to focus on my grades and the important things in my life, I became closer with God. It hasn't always been easy, but my life became so much better. It turned out everything my mom's boyfriend (now my stepdad) said was right. God provided me with love, strength and a better life. If it wasn't for Him, I might not even be here right now, so all I have to say is: Believe; put your faith in Him and rest. You will be saved in more than one way. People and friends come and go, but the Lord remains forever.

Reeve, 15

AUTHOR'S NOTE: *Reeve learned that when he put his faith in God, he was provided with a life far better than the one that he was living while using drugs. If you or one of your friends has a desire to turn away from drugs, I encourage you to talk with your parents, a counselor or a pastor. You can also contact the National Youth Crisis Hotline at 1-800-HIT-HOME (1-800-448-4663) or the National Drug Abuse Hotline at 1-800-662-4357 for support services in your area.*

... I started praying to God for strength ...

When I used to get teased, I always came back with a smart-aleck remark, making my bullies tease me even more. Every day was the same. I started getting really angry at them. I would get into fights and cause lots of trouble. I had no friends other than my twin sister. When we went into the seventh grade, I was still being picked on. I had made some friends and they got picked on, too. Finally, I had had enough, so instead of getting angry and going right back at them, I started praying to God for strength so that I could resist my desire to fight them. And slowly, I found that His strength helped me face my tough days. Now, I use kindness rather than anger. It is amazing, but I don't get picked on as much anymore, and I have great friends!

Danita, 14

So when you are troubled . . .

When I was asked for my thoughts on the strength I find in God, they came from my heart in a poem. It goes like this:

God is my strength!

The strength to love
The strength to live
The strength to forget
The strength to forgive

Strength in numbers
Strength in pairs
Strength in friends
And the lives they share

We find strength
In every nook

In a family
Or in a book

But where does the original
Strength come from?
The strength to go on
When our hearts go numb?

"Who created
This strength?" you say
God Almighty
He helps us in every way

So when you are troubled
Do not shed a tear
Turn to Him for strength
And have no fear

Saleena, 15

When I first found out, I was shocked . . .

God was strength for me when I was twelve. He is strength for me now and He will always be my strength. When I was twelve years old, my mom was diagnosed with cancer. When I first found out, I was shocked. My full-of-life, fun and joyful mom was now lifeless. In June, one day before my thirteenth birthday, my dad came home and sat down with me and my little brother and sister. Before I knew it, his eyes were filled with tears, and he was telling us that my mom wasn't in pain anymore and that even though we would all miss her, we needed to let her go. He also told us that she would always be with us, just not physically. After days of thinking and crying, I prayed to God and asked Him to help me through this. I asked Him to help me be strong for myself and for my family, and He did. Every time that I broke and cried or got stressed or angry, I thought of what my mom would have wanted and how she would want me to focus on my future. I believe God drew my thoughts to her desires to help me stay strong.

Hannah, 15

I was lost in who I was, who my family was . . .

When my parents got a divorce, I became suddenly lost. I was lost in who I was, who my family was, who my leaders in life were. With encouragement from a friend, I went to a local youth group. It was only once a week and was for about two hours. Through the group, not only did I have time away from my family troubles, but time to be with God and find out who I really was, because that was something I was really struggling with. I started praying every night. I prayed for His guidance and compassion. Slowly, I came to realize that things were getting easier and beginning to be okay. I don't know if it was just by chance that things got better when I started praying, but I really think it was because I let God know that I knew He was there and that I needed His love and guidance.

The divorce of my parents is just now final. Yet, I know that it will take a long time to get over it and accept everything that has gone on and what my parents have done to each other and our family. I think with time and the help of God, though, that He will give me the strength to make it through everything just fine and maybe come out a better person. If another teen asked me for the best piece of advice I could offer, I would have to say this: If you are trying to find out who you are, who you want to be or where you are to go in life, go and find God and talk to Him. Because it is so easy and He is always there for you. He understands what you are going through. He won't leave you like a friend might, and He is only a prayer away.

Summer, 14

When we do not have the strength to pick up our head, God will help . . .

The dictionary defines strength as being "the power to resist force," but even the strongest man has emotional weaknesses. Many times we don't have enough strength to pull through the most emotionally straining times in our lives. Yet, God is there to guide us through these times. He knows that after persevering, struggling and encountering hardships, these difficult life experiences will make us stronger in the future. This is not the physical strength described in Webster's Dictionary, but a strength defined with God's love and devotion to all of us. When we do not have the strength to pick up our head, God will help us gain enough strength to do so.

Michael, 16

He gives me the strength to face my dad . . .

Abuse. Abuse is a scary and very real word to me. I am not saying that it happens all the time, but it does happen often. Sometimes it's not always physical abuse, but it's mental abuse, too. I think what hurts the worst is that I didn't do a thing to bring on my dad's anger. It's not so much the physical abuse that hurts; it's the mental abuse. It hurts me so deeply that I become very afraid of him. He has made me so insecure about myself that I have subconsciously put up a wall around me. There are only a few special people who have gotten through this shield, and God is one of them. He has gotten past the wall because He gives me strength, courage and hope.

On the days that I just don't feel like living, He gives me the strength to do it. He gives me the strength to face my dad and the rest of the world. He gives me hope that maybe someday my dad will see how much he hurts me and stop the abuse. And maybe that will come sooner now, because most importantly, God gave me the strength to finally talk to someone about what my dad was doing. God just gives me so much that my dad doesn't or can't give me. That is one of the reasons He has gotten past my wall. I am very grateful to have God in my life. Amen!

Yolanda, 14

AUTHOR'S NOTE: *If you have ever found yourself in a situation like Yolanda's, please talk to a trusted adult. A teacher, school counselor, pastor or family friend can guide you to seek help. You can also call the National Youth Crisis Hotline at 1-800-HIT-HOME (1-800-448-4663) or the National Clearinghouse on Child Abuse and Neglect at 1-800-394-3366 for guidance, support and referrals. Know that no one deserves to be abused and that it is an individual's right as a human being to be safe. Also, Yolanda suggests that on some days she just doesn't feel like living. Please refer back to the "T" Talk in chapter 3 for reassurance and guidance that suicide is not the answer. And again, if you have ever contemplated suicide, I encourage you to seek comfort and courage from God and find the strength in Him to talk to someone about what you are feeling.*

. . . His strength can be our strength

"Put some muscle into that, boy!" "I expect you to have enough strength to lift that weight!" or "Put your back into it!" are all ways of saying that you need to put effort and strength into whatever it is that you are doing. There are two different kinds of strength, though. There is man's strength and then there is God's strength. God didn't intend for people to carry their burdens by themselves. God wants all of us to know that His strength can be our strength. When we dwell in God's strength, we receive grace, love and forgiveness. God gives us strength in our lives when we face new challenges, when we doubt or are depressed. Often we can find His strength through prayer. When we pray, it gives God a chance to comfort us and guide us through our trials. So look to God for strength. He works in mysterious ways and will build you up when you are lifting a heavy load!

Jasmine, 14

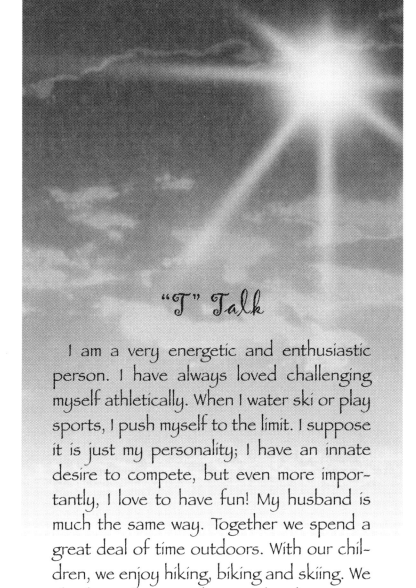

"T" Talk

I am a very energetic and enthusiastic person. I have always loved challenging myself athletically. When I water ski or play sports, I push myself to the limit. I suppose it is just my personality; I have an innate desire to compete, but even more importantly, I love to have fun! My husband is much the same way. Together we spend a great deal of time outdoors. With our children, we enjoy hiking, biking and skiing. We also love to camp. When my daughter was a little over one and my son was three years old, my husband and I took them camping. The campground was dry and very dirty, but we had a fantastic time. I think our daughter ate more dirt that weekend than she did food! Little did I know that our fun-filled camping trip would change my life.

Over a month later, I began to feel sick. At first I thought I had the flu. I was nauseous and fatigued. Throughout the next few months, I lost weight, muscle tone, strength and experienced difficulty breathing. Anything that I did that took muscle exertion left me breathless. As active as I normally was, I was devastated by my physical condition, and I was terrified that something was seriously wrong with me. I visited many doctors, but they were baffled by my condition. At one point, a specialist at a nationally acclaimed diagnostic institute patted me on the back and suggested that I was overstressed. I left there not knowing if I should cry and scream or commit myself to a psychiatric ward. People who know me call me an eternal optimist, but at that point I became depressed. I didn't have the strength to be the mom and wife that I had always been, and no doctor could tell me what was wrong. I began to doubt myself and my symptoms.

Tragically, as my body deteriorated, I feared that I was dying. Finally, after six months, I saw another specialist who diagnosed me with Lyme disease, a bacteria that replicates as it invades your body systems and renders them useless. Apparently, a tick bit me when we were camping. The tick carried Lyme and passed it on to me. After five long years of treatment, I feel very blessed to be in excellent health today. Yet, I am also aware that my faith in God and my belief that He would be with me gave me the strength and courage to persevere. I am cognizant, too, of the many valuable lessons that God taught me through my illness. One encounter, in particular, reinforced the power of God's presence in my life.

It was a beautiful winter day as I traveled along a mountain road to meet my husband for lunch at a local ski resort. My body was quite weak and I had yet to be diagnosed, but I was grateful to be getting out and enjoying the day. As my children slept in the back seat, I drove along listening to the radio, when all of a sudden my right hand began to feel tingly, as if little needles were prickling my fingers and the palm of my hand. As the feeling progressed up my forearm, my fingers began to involuntarily curl into a tight fist. I began to feel afraid, not knowing what was happening to my body and very aware that if something happened to me, my kids would be alone and unprotected in the car. Suddenly, my right arm contracted and began to curl into my body. My left arm also began to follow the same pattern, tingling, contracting and becoming useless. I feared that perhaps it was the altitude that was causing this episode, so I thought I should try to head back down the mountain. Even with the full use of one's hands, it would be a difficult turn to make under winter conditions. To my right was a huge wall of snow and to my left a sheer drop-off. Ice coated the road in an invisible sheet. But at that point, I felt that turning around was my only hope. I was beginning to feel the same tingling sensation in my face, and both of my hands now seemed glued to my chest. Without the benefit of my hands or forearms, I used my elbows and chest to turn my car around and guide it to the side of the road. I was unable to put my car into park and feared for my children's safety, sure that I would soon lose consciousness. With my foot on the brake, I waved my elbow out the window hoping someone would stop to help me, though no one did.

I was frustrated, helpless and afraid when I realized I hadn't yet asked the only one who could help me. God knew my situation, and He was near. I prayed with all of my heart for God to give me the strength to hold on and to please have the next person stop. I also remember asking the Lord to let it be a good person, someone who would help me and protect my children. And He did. In fact, He sent two people in the next car. They reminded me of my parents, as the man got into my car and drove my children and me safely to an emergency room. His wife followed us and then made sure the kids were taken care of until my family arrived.

I later learned that the bacteria from the Lyme disease had attacked my respiratory system and ultimately caused that reaction in my body. But through that experience, the life lesson that I learned was most precious. I was reminded that God is always near, yet sometimes we forget to call on Him for help. He knows when we are afraid or hurting. If we turn to Him when we are troubled, He will comfort us with His strength.

Because I am a very independent person, I often try to control many situations in my life. Even when I am failing miserably, I stubbornly persist and usually watch things get worse. But when I let go and realize that, in fact, I don't have to be in control because God is, that is when things seem to work out. It is difficult for Him to take care of me unless I allow Him to. Just like on the mountain, I couldn't make people stop to help me, but God could. I had to get beyond myself and my control to let God help me.

I don't believe that God caused my Lyme disease, but I do know that I have grown spiritually because of my encounter with Lyme. God has taught me and touched my life in so many ways through the disease, but when I was initially sick and undiagnosed, I couldn't see it.

I think that most people have experienced a time when life doesn't make sense. Have you experienced a trial in your life that left you feeling overwhelmed and unsure? Maybe like some of the teens who wrote for this chapter, your situation is severe and you feel as if your world has collapsed around you. What can you do? Rely on God's promise to pull you through. The Bible says that God is our rock, that if we rely on Him, He will be there. If we lay our fears and confusion on the foundation of God's love, He will give us the strength to persevere through our most challenging life situations. Do you remember the story from the Old Testament about David and Goliath? David knew that he could conquer Goliath because he understood that he would not face the giant alone. David knew with certainty that God would guide him and keep him safe. His courage flourished in the knowledge that God was with him.

If, like Yolanda, who shared her encounter with abuse, you, too, have had a similar experience, God can give you the strength to seek help. It is important that you do this because you do not in any way deserve to be abused. In fact, it is your right to be safe. It may be scary to reach out on your own for help, but with God beside you, you can do anything. Go talk to an adult whom you trust, like a teacher, pastor or school counselor. Let God take you by the hand and lead you there, because you are His child and He wants you to be safe. Let God pour courage upon your soul and give you the strength to protect yourself.

At the same time, perhaps the problems that you deal with in your life aren't extreme, like some of those you just read about. As a teacher and speaker, teens often come to me to talk about their problems and, although this chapter addresses very sensitive issues, most teenagers deal with dilemmas that are less intense. Many teens feel overwhelmed with school, sports, activities or work. Others get disappointed with friendships or boyfriend-girlfriend relationships. Some teenagers feel frustrated when their parents don't seem to understand their problems or when their younger siblings invade their space. Perhaps you can relate to these issues. If so, please know that God is there to provide you with strength, too. The fact that your problem may not involve an extreme situation doesn't mean that you shouldn't call on the Lord for support and strength. The Bible tells us that God always wants us to call on Him. No problem is too big or too small for God because He loves us.

Extraordinarily, the power in His love breeds hope in our lives and gives us this strength. As a teen, your life can be very confusing, emotional and lonely. It can also be fun, exciting and filled with friends. Let God be one of your friends. Let Him share your life and bring you strength!

CHAPTER FIVE

In You I Trust!

Trusting God
is that essential . . .

$\mathcal{I}$f you are reading this book in sequence and have just completed chapters 3 and 4, then you know that various teens shared their most serious trials and tragedies. Although frequently people believe in God because they are brought up in a family of believers, sometimes it takes an extreme situation to lead others to their spiritual convictions. For these people, putting their trust in the Lord may be the only thing that gives them hope for their future. Trusting God is that essential. Throughout this chapter, teens share their philosophies of trust. You may be one who has put your trust in God since you were a young child. Or perhaps, your relation-ship with God is recently evolving. Regardless, I believe you will find this chapter both enlightening and insightful. Take heart and trust in the Lord!

Mrs. T

After I talk to God about something, I feel like . . .

Throughout my life, I have always had a hard time trusting others. Not because everyone in my life is not trustworthy, but because I have just been afraid to trust them. I am afraid of people breaking my confidence or making fun of me for what I have told them. Of course, throughout my life, I have found a few people who I can trust, but there is only one person I can trust completely. This person is God. I know that whatever I have to say, He will listen to it, and whatever I have done, He will not make fun of me. I know that I will always be able to go to Him for help with anything. I do not have to worry about Him telling others. I can tell God anything, unlike with some of the people in my life, where I am only able to share some things with them. Being able to trust God completely has helped me *greatly in my life. When there is no one in your life who you can talk to and trust, then all your feelings and emotions will just build up inside you, and this can cause many problems in your life. But if you are able to trust someone with anything you say or do, then it is easier to work your problems out. After I talk to God about something, I feel like I don't have to worry about it anymore. Many times, if you don't tell someone about something you may be worried about, then it will get even worse. Luckily, though, I have found that by talking to God about something, it makes it easier to deal with. I hope that for the rest of my life I will keep this complete trust that I have in God, and I hope that others will be able to find this trust in Him as I have.*

Belinda, 17

. . . when I feel like no one trusts me, God always does . . .

Why don't my parents trust me? This is the question I ask myself every day. My parents tell me that trust needs to be earned, but what I don't understand is how I am supposed to earn their trust if they don't trust me to do things to prove that I can. I always wondered if other teens have to go through the trust things with their parents, too, or if it's just because I am the oldest. Who knows? But I do know that when I feel like no one trusts me, God always does and I can always trust God. Sometimes I just want to tell my parents all the stuff that goes on in my life and know that they would understand. It doesn't always work out that way. That's why I trust God with my problems and secrets, because I know He won't think less of me; He will just love me. I also know that whatever I tell Him is between me and

Him. Being able to tell Him things, trust Him and believe in Him makes our relationship special.

Ashlyn, 14

When these situations occur, I turn to God . . .

Have you ever felt that no one trusts you? I have, and believe me it stinks. I have had a few experiences where someone doesn't trust me, although it hurts more when it is someone you really care about. My parents are very good to me, but sometimes when situations occur that don't seem normal, they tend to ask questions because they think I might be doing something that they might not approve of. I know my parents love me, but because they are so strict, I think they must not trust me. Here is a typical story that would occur: I would ask my parents to go to a friend's for the evening. They then would ask me questions like, "Are his parents home?" and "Will there be any drugs or alcohol?" I, myself, do not do drugs or drink; however, they always seem to give me the third

*degree. I have also had situations where my girl-
friends didn't trust me even though I am the most
faithful guy. When these situations occur, I turn
to God to help me understand why people are the
way they are. Sometimes when things get stressful, I sit and talk to God so that He may guide
me, because I trust Him.*

Seth, 18

God will never leave my side . . .

Whenever anything isn't as good as I want it to be, such as my grades or my relationships with my parents or friends, I know that I can always turn to God. It often feels like I have nobody to trust when it comes to the problems in my life. But I do know that no matter what is going wrong or how bad things seem to get, I always can trust that God will be there. He will never leave my side, and for that, I am thankful.

Donna, 15

*... I reserve my serious stuff
for God ...*

I believe in God and trust Him more than anyone else. I trust Him with whatever I say,
because He does not judge me or give me a
remark or a "look" whenever I tell Him something. I trust Him because He won't go and tell
everyone what I have said. He does not judge me
or yell at me if I have done something wrong. I
have friends whom I can talk to about problems,
and I have great parents. Sometimes, though,
they look at me and seem like they are thinking,
"What is wrong with him?" That is why I think it
is easier to trust God a little more than friends
and family.

I have learned from trusting God that I can get
through different obstacles in life. If no one listens, I can always turn to God. And I learned
that sometimes when I tell other people things

because of how they might respond, I hold some things back. That is when I turn to God. I find it easier putting my trust in Him, because He does not respond directly with words, as my friends and family would. I think that I like it when people just listen and don't respond by asking tons of questions. But rarely do people do this. If I were to talk to someone about a serious problem, I know that they would just jump right in with questions and advice. So, I reserve my serious stuff for God because of TRUST.

Jamal, 14

He will never betray me . . .

I have chosen to trust God, because He is always there for me when I need Him the most. He will never betray me, and He is always behind me no matter what. Even when I stray from God, He will always accept me back. I can trust God in any situation. He is the one true friend who I know will never, ever dislike me or not accept me. No matter how far I stray from Him, He forgives me and accepts me back. He is the one, true trustworthy friend that someone could have. I tell all teens: "You should have your own relationship with this perfect friend because He is only going to help you, never hurt you."

Justin, 15

. . . we can't just turn to God and say, "Tell everyone to trust me"

Why do most teens complain that their parents don't trust them? Maybe it's because they haven't earned their parents' trust. Most teens lie to get away with the things that they do. I know because I have been there. But if just once teens could open their hearts and let God come into their lives, then maybe they wouldn't feel like lying so much and then their parents would trust them. Not only that, but also as teens we have to earn trust, because we can't just turn to God and say, "Tell everyone to trust me." We can't do that. But we can tell the truth. That helps a lot. We would get respect from telling the truth and with God's help get the trust back from our parents.

Dee Jay, 14

I have no clue as to what I would be like . . .

Throughout the years of my life, I have been guided to trust God. Today I am old enough not to be guided anymore. I now choose to trust God. I trust God in many ways. I trust Him to guide me through my everyday life, to be there when I need comfort and to direct me in doing what is right. Another simple reason why I put my trust in God is because I believe that He truthfully knows what is right for me. I have no clue as to what I would be like if I did not trust God. God has protected me from major injuries, drugs and from me turning away from Him. He has taught me to love myself and, in doing so, I can share my love with other people. I have also learned to trust other people besides myself. In setting a good example for others, I have seen the effects it can have on someone. People my age tend to look up to me because I seem upbeat and kind-hearted. I usually don't get on someone's bad side, but when I do, I turn to God and ask Him why I made that person angry. When I talk to God or pray to Him, I don't always hope for an answer. I hope that I can learn from my mistakes by talking them out with God. So, again I do trust God to be there when I am down or need to reason something out. He is an inspiration to me and I look forward to the future because of my trust in Him.

Dereck, 16

Since then, I have not trusted anyone completely . . .

A few years ago, I told one of my close friends a personal secret and expected him not to tell anyone. Instead, I found out that he had told most of my friends. I felt betrayed by the friend and by God for letting this happen to me. Since then, I have not trusted anyone completely, except for God. I know I said that I felt as if He had betrayed me, but really He didn't. I realized God had nothing to do with my choice to think that I could trust someone with something I should have only confided to God. From the day I realized God was someone I could trust, I have told Him everything, and He listens! There isn't a day that I don't turn to Him at least once. I learned a valuable lesson, too; no matter what you tell God, whether it is bad, good or *indifferent, He won't tell anyone, no matter how hard they beg.*

Connor, 18

I guess I have always been afraid . . .

I am an eleventh-grade student—the kind of student that a teacher will see walk by and say, "Oh, I know her, she is a good kid." But no one who said that ever really knew me. I could never open up to anyone to let them get to know me. I guess I have always been afraid of being hurt. I have gone into meaningless friendships and entangling relationships, and come out hurt and deceived. The one who has never let me down, though, is God. He has been my constant. I have always believed in Him, although sometimes in different measures, and He has always been there—the one to trust, care for and love me. By having my constant, I have realized that I do need to do my part. Even if I still have difficulty trusting people, it doesn't mean that I can't let people trust me. You can never be a good con-stant unless you're Christlike, and so I have made that part of my goal, to strive to be a good constant just like God.

Sherry, 17

God is like a best friend . . .

Trust is a hard topic. As I have found, once you have broken someone's trust in you, it is difficult for that person to build it back up. Although issues like that have happened to me, it hasn't affected the way that I trust others or God. God is like a best friend. He is really good at listening, and a person can tell Him anything without the whole school knowing the next day. You know He will forgive you for what you have done, no matter what. People put a lot of trust in God, letting Him guide us and help us make the right decisions. From God, I have learned to trust in people and also forgive. More importantly, I have learned to use God as an example and to be more trustworthy.

Nessa, 18

I have never done anything to cause . . .

No one ever said that being a teen was easy, but I never expected it to be this hard. I never expected a lot of things, least of all a lack of trust from my parents. It's tough to deal with. Authority is necessary, but it can also be frustrating. I have never done anything to cause my parents' doubt, and yet I am still treated with no trust. This tells me that they therefore do not respect how I feel about things. In another sense, however, I can see where they are coming from. I can understand their need to keep me close by them. After all, I will be leaving home for college in a few years and they don't want to see me get hurt. Oddly enough, when I feel too stifled or mistrusted by my parents, I feel that I can turn to God and be trusted. I know deep inside that He trusts me and my judgment. He guides me, as well, and it is because of Him that I am able to trust that everything will work itself out.

Jaqulin, 14

. . . I know I can trust God

Even though I can't see Him, I know I can trust God. He listens to me and doesn't make judgments. He hears what I say and just lets me talk. Sometimes it's a big comfort to know that the person you're pouring your heart out to won't give you a lecture or think you're weird.

Riley, 15

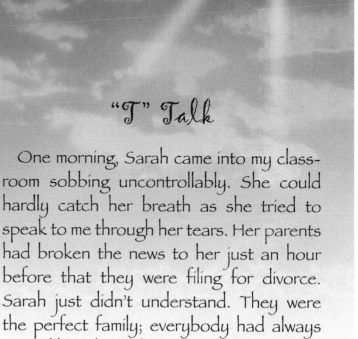

"T" Talk

One morning, Sarah came into my classroom sobbing uncontrollably. She could hardly catch her breath as she tried to speak to me through her tears. Her parents had broken the news to her just an hour before that they were filing for divorce. Sarah just didn't understand. They were the perfect family; everybody had always teased her about that. They had never had any problems. She rarely, if ever, saw them argue. So why would they be getting a divorce?

Apparently, her mom had fallen in love with another man. She was moving out and leaving Sarah, her little sister and her dad in order to live with this man. Sarah could not believe that her mom would betray her dad this way. But what hurt more was that she felt her mom had deceived her, too. Isn't it just a given, Sarah asked me, that every teenage girl should have a mom there to talk to? How could her mom choose another man over her family? Sarah had always naturally trusted that her mom would be there for her. How could she just walk away? Now, she didn't know if she could ever trust again.

Sarah's story is not uncommon. Many teens have experienced situations in which someone has shattered their trust. Trust is a fragile bridge that brings people together. But because it is delicate, it can easily be destroyed. Unfortunately, when this happens, it often leaves people hanging on by a thread, feeling confused, hopeless and sometimes even angry.

Have you ever felt like you're barely holding on, shocked by a betrayal? Perhaps, like Sarah, you had always believed that your parents would stay committed to each other and remain the foundation for your family. Yet, here they are, divorcing. Or maybe it is your friends who broke your trust. Suppose they betrayed your confidence or talked about you behind your back. If such an incident has occurred in your life, it might be difficult for you to trust again. Many teens have told me, "Mrs. T, I am not going to let myself get burned twice." They feel that it is easier to stay away from friendships or guard their emotions around family members, rather than set themselves up for heartache. The sadness in this philosophy is that in choosing not to trust, teens risk missing out on love and joy, friendships and fun.

Or sometimes it goes much deeper. Take the two students who entered their school, shot several of their classmates and a teacher, then killed themselves. Apparently, they felt betrayed as a result of years of being teased and taunted, and they began to isolate themselves. They trusted no one. It makes me so sad to think that if there would have been just one person that they could have trusted enough to talk to, perhaps the senseless and tragic murders could have been prevented.

In all the years that I have worked with teenagers, one issue that continues to recur is the concept of trust. Teens talk about trust as a value that they hold very close to their hearts. They treasure trust and do anything possible to protect it. If someone damages or deceives this trust, it is as if they are breaking the person's heart. You may have experienced this type of betrayal and know what it feels like. As much as your parents, siblings or friends may not intend to break your heart or shatter your trust, occasionally it happens. During these times you may feel as if you can trust no one. Well, take heart! There is someone you can always trust: God. He never turns away from you or breaks His promises. God is always listening and constantly available. At times when we feel so alone, all we have to do is call on Him and He is there.

I often think about the disciples when they were out on the sea in their little fishing boat. A storm came from out of nowhere as it often does at sea. They were so afraid. I would guess that they felt helpless and alone. And then, without fail, up walks Jesus. Yes, you read it right. They are in the middle of the sea and here comes Jesus walking on water, calming not only the sea, but the disciples' fears, as well. I'm sure that once they realized that it was really Him and He had come to save them, they must have asked themselves, "Why didn't we trust? He told us He would always be here. He asked us to trust Him, so why didn't we?"

My parents experienced a similar situation. They were in their sailboat, sailing south toward Mexico, when they encountered a storm. The waves were huge and my mom and dad were still inexperienced sailors. It was my mom's turn on night watch and she was terrified. Yet, in the midst of the storm God was near. My mom prayed throughout her watch, but as the storm grew, she felt that her prayers came secondary to her fright. After two hours, my dad took over watch, and my mom went below. She tried to get some rest, but as she listened to the sounds of the water crashing against the hull, panic set in and she imagined the boat breaking into little pieces, leaving her and my dad to drown.

So, she continued to pray. As her fear heightened, my mom began to realize that she had absolutely no control of their current situation. She couldn't calm the storm. She had no authority over the ocean as it thrashed their vessel from wave to wave. Only in that moment did she understand that she had to completely surrender her usual need for control and put her trust in God. She prayed, "Okay, God, I'm afraid and I'm not able to feel brave, so please take care of the sea and calm it down."

As Jesus demonstrated with the disciples, He has the power to do such things. Within moments of my mom's prayer, the noise of the storm began to quiet and the relentless waves became still. My mom has always believed in the influence of prayer, but this absolute and virtually immediate response from God caused *her* to feel humble and appreciative of His power. He calmed my mother's fears, as well as the sea, and reminded her that although some situations will be out of her control, if she chooses to trust God, He will be there.

Like my mom, many of us have the need to control various circumstances in our lives. We like to take hold of the reins and assert direction and command. This gives us a sense of order that makes us feel safe and secure. However, when things happen in our lives that cause the reins to be ripped from our hands, it creates chaos and confusion within us. This is why it is so important to place our trust in God. When it comes right down to it, He is truly the one in control. When we try to dominate every facet of our lives, we are, in essence, trying to dominate God. Eventually, though, instead of feeling peaceful, we will feel frustration, disappointment or anger when circumstances don't turn out as we've planned. Yet, if we set our daily worries and blessings at God's feet and choose to trust in Him, He promises to guide and comfort us.

Jesus makes this commitment to you, personally. He only asks that you trust Him. Let Him calm your fears and still your storms. God is with you always. If you "let go, and let God," as the old saying goes, He will direct your path and never leave you alone. Without a doubt, there will be situations in your life that are completely out of your control, as Sarah learned when her mother left. Although she couldn't change the current upheaval in her family, if she had let go and let God comfort her, she may have felt more peace.

In addition, if you are one who has difficulty trusting others, I pray that when you experience the peacefulness and comfort that fills your heart when you trust the Lord, you will have the confidence to trust others as well. With God by your side, I pray that you will open your heart and experience the love and joy that relationships can bring when you entrust yourself to others. I think you may find that when you do this, they will trust you as well. It is a wonderful feeling and a valuable gift. God will help you along the way; just put your trust in Him. Lord, in You I trust!

CHAPTER SIX

God, How Could You Let This Happen?!

. . . God is waiting patiently . . .

Have you ever asked God, "How could you let this happen?" I know many teenagers, as well as adults, who have. Sometimes situations occur in our lives that we don't understand. They can leave us feeling confused, frustrated or even angry. Occasionally, people blame God for the injustices or cruelties of life. I included this chapter in *Teens Talkin' Faith* because I wanted you to know that if you have ever felt angry at God, you are not alone. You will find teen contributors who share that they have felt much the same way. However, I also wanted you to recognize that God is waiting patiently and lovingly for you to realize that blaming Him for life's tragedies or frustrations is not the answer. Instead, when you turn to God for guidance and reassurance, He will open your heart and your eyes to understanding, acceptance and hope.

Mrs. T

Why did I blame God for my mother's illness?

Breast cancer is a terrible disease that many women suffer from. Sometimes there is a cure for it, but will a person be cured emotionally from dealing with it? Why did God have to give it to my mother? What did I ever do to make Him punish my mother? These are the questions I constantly asked myself when my mother was diagnosed with breast cancer. The moment my mom told me that she was really sick and needed an operation, a wave of anger came over me. It wasn't toward my mom or my dad or even myself; it was toward God. Why did I blame God for my mother's illness? To this day, I still don't know. Maybe it was that I could yell at Him, and He wouldn't yell back. Or maybe I was just looking for a scapegoat. Or perhaps it simply just felt right. For whatever reason, I was mad. I only went to church because my family made me. My mom insisted that I had to thank God for her recovery, but all I could think of was, "We wouldn't have to pray for her recovery if He didn't make her sick in the first place!" Soon I realized that it was silly to think this way and to hate God. God helped my mother recover, and she is well now, which is all the more reason to apologize to God and love Him with every part of my heart.

Staci, 18

How can a mother, who has cared for her child for ten years, just walk . . .

The events of that Sunday morning in March are still fresh in my mind. We had gone to church like always, where my mom was my Sunday school teacher. On this particular Sunday, a friend of mine had come with us. The details aren't so important, but I remember that the car ride home seemed to take forever. I remember a lot of screaming and yelling between my mom and my dad, and a lot of curse words, too. After that car ride, my mom was gone. I was ten years old, but my mother was gone and starting a new life without me. How can a mother, who has cared for her child for ten years, just walk away one day? I still don't know.

That was a very traumatic day for me. It turned my life upside down. I was really depressed, as were my dad and sister. So as my *only remaining family, they couldn't help me. My friends, who were as young and stupid as I was, had no idea what to say. I was alone, so I turned to God. The hurt wouldn't go away, though. I prayed and prayed, but I was still alone. That's when I stopped depending on God. He let me down. He let something bad happen to me. My faith went straight down the tubes. I was so mad at God. I got new friends who were in the same parental situation as I was in, and I stopped believing. For three years, I was Godless. Whether it was puberty, a new school or my faithlessness, I had a whole new personality. I changed so much, and mostly for the worst. I didn't go to church in those three years, nor did I pray. I was lost, and I really didn't care. But then last year, I realized that my new life was failing me. It left me empty inside. Slowly, I began to have a desire to find God again. Recently, I have been more complete than since my mom left. It has been a long journey, but I am glad I am not mad at God anymore and that I have Him in my life again.*

Shane, 15

I was so confused, hurt and angry . . .

Ah, the teenage years . . . a time when nothing is what it seems to be. Something right is now suddenly wrong, and everything changes. Who helps along the way? Friends and family can only do so much since they do not know exactly what you're going through. God does know, though. He takes every step and breath with everyone. When my uncle died from cancer, my immediate reaction was to blame God. I was so confused, hurt and angry. As time passed, God unclogged my mind. I was no longer angry or confused. God simply had a better place for my uncle to go. On Earth, there are hardships, but in heaven everything is happy. Why would I want to stop my uncle from going to a better place? I still have a lot of questions about death. Maybe as I grow older they will be answered, and then again maybe they won't. All I know is that God *is a great listener. Sometimes He even lets me throw a punch or two.*

Kerri, 17

I blamed God for all the pain . . .

I think God is patient because every time
something goes bad or wrong, I most likely get
angry. When I was little I would blame God for
all the bad and depressing times. I was often
depressed and sad because I was adopted when
I was a baby, and I just didn't quite fit in all that
well. I had some kids whom I was close to, but it
was hard for me to make many friends. Some
people made fun of me because of my race,
which didn't make it any easier. I blamed God
for all the pain and hurt I had to go through, but
later I began to trust Him. Sometimes I still get
depressed, but I just think of all the good things.
For example, today I have a loving family, good
friends, a house and lots of other good things to
come.

Ragena, 14

After realizing it wasn't God's purpose to hurt me . . .

When I was in the seventh grade, I had a painful and sad experience. I was only twelve years old, and my grandmother died. At this time, I didn't really understand what was going on, because it was the first time someone close had died in my life. My grandmother and I had a close relationship, and we were "best buds." She always understood everything I did or said and was behind me no matter what it was. So the day I got called home from school and found out my grandmother died, I became really upset and angry at God. I was angry at God because I felt that He took someone I was close to away from me and hurt others around me, like my mom. After realizing it wasn't God's purpose to hurt me, and that death is just part of life, I slowly gained back my friendship with Him by talking to my grandmother in heaven through praying to God. It was a slow process to gain my respect and love back for God, but now I feel like He is my "best bud."

Steven, 17

. . . I got mad at God and stopped praying . . .

As I lay in bed thinking about tomorrow, I hear the front door shut. In walks my brother, drunker than ever. He is so loud that he wakes up my parents. I hear them yelling at each other. Then, he says something mean and walks out the door. I hear my mom start to cry. Every night we go through the same thing over and over again. Sometimes the pain of knowing what he is doing to himself and the danger he is putting himself in is unbearable. All I want to do is lock myself in my room and cry. But I don't. I somehow get through it. If only he knew that every night he doesn't come home, I expect a phone call from the hospital telling us that he is in critical condition. I couldn't stand to live without him. He had been my role model for so many years, but then he began to change.

About a year ago, I began to pray every night for him, and every Sunday that I went to church I prayed for him. One night I thought to myself, "This isn't working; what good is this doing?" So I got mad at God and stopped praying, but things only got worse. So I decided that maybe, just maybe, if I started praying again, it would get better slowly. Well, ever since I have been praying again, things have gradually gotten better. Before, my brother didn't even take the word "job" to mind, and now he has one. Even though he still drinks, I think he is getting much better. I used to not believe that God would actually listen to what I had to say, but now I know that He does and He will help. I just hope that one day my brother will see that his drinking is not the way and that he will get some serious help. I can only pray that this day will be soon. God has given me the strength and the hope to deal with my brother and help him through these times. Sometimes I think that when my brother looks at me, he wants to stop drinking but can't because he has gotten himself hooked. I pray that he will find God someday and understand what he is putting himself and our family through.

Stephanie, 14

I was angry and thought that all her prayers and devotion to God went unanswered . . .

Last June, I lost a close aunt to a two-year gru-eling battle with cancer. When she died I thought, "How could God let her leave her family? She has children and a husband. Why would He take her away?" She was a true believer and loved God very much. She would even get choked up when we would talk about God because she loved Him with her whole mind, body and spirit. After loving Him this much, it enraged me that she died. I was angry and thought that all her prayers and devotion to God went unanswered. It was almost like He wasn't listening to her pleas for healing. In time, I real-ized He did answer her prayers, just in a differ-ent way. He healed her by bringing her home with Him, and that me wanting her back here on

Earth was selfish. It was okay that she wasn't here because she wasn't in pain anymore. I think everyone gets mad with God, and it is amazing how He will always be there for us even when we are angry with Him.

Rita, 16

... I found myself doubting God and being very angry ...

My faith in God has always been an important factor in my life, and it has always been very strong. However, last year my beliefs were put to a test. Twelve years of religious school could not prepare me for the gravest experience of my life. Last year, a week before Thanksgiving, my cousin committed suicide. He was sixteen years old, the same age as me. His death came as a complete shock to my entire family. Even though my faith had always been strong, I found myself doubting God and being very angry with Him. I couldn't believe that the same God who had delivered so many blessings to me previously could tear my life apart by taking someone I loved away from me at such a young age. This was a very difficult, stressful time in my life. I am very lucky to have a family, teachers and friends who have been supportive through this time. Through a lot of thinking and prayer, my faith in God has been restored. I still feel anger when I think about my cousin, but I have grown to understand that God was not punishing me, and I need His guidance and support to get through these tough times.

Jillian, 17

AUTHOR'S NOTE: Remember, if you or someone you know is contemplating suicide, it is so important to reach out for help. Jillian's cousin made a choice to take his own life. It was a choice he didn't have to make. Parents, pastors, counselors, teachers or family friends would be the best people to talk to, or you could call the National Suicide Hotline at 1-800-SUICIDE (1-800-784-2433).

... I didn't understand why He had to take away my mother

When I was little I knew about God, and I thought that the only reason people prayed to Him was when they needed help. I never knew that you could just pray to Him if you were having a bad day and needed someone to listen. I would pray about things like making up with friends after a fight or finding a lost pet. I always made up with friends and I always found my lost pet, so I thought that God was the greatest. Then, when my mom died about four years ago, I was angry with God because I didn't understand why He had to take away my mother. It wasn't fair that all my friends had moms and I didn't. I didn't think that He was the greatest, and I never prayed anymore.

Four years later, I started to talk to someone about my mom's death because I was having a *hard time with it. She asked me about my faith, and I had no answer. I mean, I still believed in God and heaven, but it wasn't the same as when I was little. I think I was still really mad at Him. She brought up faith a lot, though, and I always felt weird because I hadn't thought about it in a long time. Then when she said she would pray for me, it made me think,* Why couldn't I pray for myself? *I started to pray to God and asked Him to help me. After that, I felt a little bit more reassurance and comfort. So, I started to pray more often. It started to feel really good. I stopped praying to Him only for help, and started just to talk and tell Him what was going on in my life. Although I still miss my mom, I am not angry anymore, because now I know God is the greatest!*

Marissa, 15

My brother was arrested twice more . . .

My older brother and I had been pretty close. We used to go to youth group and just hang out. I had always been very strong in my faith and had recently been baptized. One night, I was holding my brother's jacket when a packet of cigarettes fell out. I was shocked. I wondered why my brother was smoking and why he was hiding it. After that, my brother started getting into bad stuff. I asked God to help my brother to stop and to help me be strong. On my brother's seventeenth birthday, he went out with some friends. My parents asked him to be home by 11:00. At two in the morning, I heard my mom crying. I got up, and she told me that my brother had been arrested for use of marijuana, driving under the influence and curfew violation. I was so upset. How could God let this happen to him?

I wondered how He could let my brother do something so bad.

After that, I started to get mad at God, and I turned away from Him. My brother was arrested twice more. I was so mad at God, I could barely stand it. Then I started talking to my youth pastor. He helped me to realize that maybe God was showing me that sometimes people just make bad choices and that poor choices have consequences. I then understood that this is why my brother had gotten arrested, and it wasn't God's fault. I learned that God didn't deserve my blame, and I began to trust Him again.

Danielle, 14

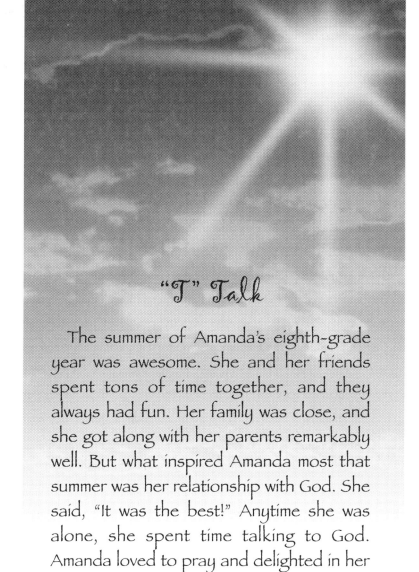

"J" Talk

The summer of Amanda's eighth-grade year was awesome. She and her friends spent tons of time together, and they always had fun. Her family was close, and she got along with her parents remarkably well. But what inspired Amanda most that summer was her relationship with God. She said, "It was the best!" Anytime she was alone, she spent time talking to God. Amanda loved to pray and delighted in her weekly youth group. She valued her faith, her family and her life.

But when school started, Amanda's perspective shifted. She said everything changed—her looks, personality, friends, family and especially her relationship with God. Amanda felt that her friends had turned on her, and rumors were being spread about her that weren't true. To compound that, school was more difficult than it had been in the past, and her grades dropped. It seemed like everybody was on her case, especially her parents, and Amanda began to feel that her life was worthless. As the stresses in her life became overwhelming, Amanda turned away from God. Instead of spending her time alone, praying as she had done in the past, Amanda became consumed with thoughts of suicide. Each night she would think about how she would end her life, telling herself that everyone would be happier if she was gone. She knew deep down that suicide wasn't the answer to her problems, but she was so focused on herself and her needs that she couldn't see beyond to the hope of the future.

In addition, the one whom she later realized she should have been turning to, she blamed. Amanda was intensely angry with God. She accused Him repeatedly, saying, "God, why do You let me feel this hurt? Why are You doing this to me? I can't believe You, God. All my problems are Your fault!" As Amanda's anger at God grew, so did her plans to take her life. On the night that she had promised herself that she would end her life, Amanda was alone in her room. Suddenly, she felt someone grab her, but when she turned to look to see who it was, no one was there. With that, she fell to the floor, sobbing. Amanda finally understood that she didn't want to end her life; she just wanted her problems to go away. Mostly, Amanda felt enlightened by an unfailing belief that it was God who stopped her. Amanda eventually realized that God was with her the whole time. He didn't want her to die, and He knew that deep down inside, she didn't want to take her life either.

Amanda came to understand that had she turned to God with her problems instead of blaming Him for the trials in her life, He could have guided and comforted her. Amanda's youth pastor helped her to understand that it wasn't God who had turned on her; it was Amanda who had shut herself off from God. Yet, God accepted Amanda's anger. Perhaps He shows such mercy because He can identify. Remember the account in the gospel where Jesus goes into the temple of God and overturns the tables of those who were using such a holy place to buy and sell goods? When I think of someone overturning tables, I imagine rage. I assume Jesus was angry that the house of His Father was being used for trade instead of prayer, worship and healing. So although Amanda shunned God and placed the anger towards her life situation on Him, God understood. He waited patiently while Amanda figured this out, and as she learned, He never left her side.

Perhaps you have experienced a time in your life when you have been angry with God. If so, know that you are not alone. Like any situation in which there is pain and heartache, it is typical to try to place the blame for the injustice on a specific entity. Often, that entity is God. It is quite common to blame God for life's inequities. After all, we frequently blame Him because we believe in Him. The wonderful thing about God is that He loves us so much, He is willing to take the blame. But really, He doesn't deserve it. It is true that there are many things that happen in our lives that don't seem fair. For example, if someone we love gets cancer, it just doesn't seem right. We feel fearful and angry, and God is a perfect target for our outrage. However, I don't believe He caused the cancer. Nor do I presume that God wants to see us in physical or emotional pain. I do believe, though, that our time on this Earth is a personal and spiritual journey in which we grow from everything that we experience. I think that God can use the situations in our lives to teach us valuable lessons.

For example, during spring break of my sister Jaime's sophomore year in college, she and some classmates traveled to Mexico for a week of missionary work. They had worked all year planning for the event and were very excited. Following their arrival, they worked together the first few days to build homes for people who lived there, in addition to providing other missionary services. Each morning they would get up, share a breakfast together and then pile into the few cars that they had to get to the worksites. In the small amount of spare time they had, they took time to pray, sing praises and have fun! One day, while traveling to that day's destination, one of the vehicles carrying five students was hit head-on by another car. Three kids were killed. These teenagers were on a mission, doing God's work and they were killed. It just didn't make sense to me. My sister and the others spent the next few days dealing with the tragedy and finishing their work.

When I spoke with Jaime after the accident, I asked her if she was mad at God. I felt mad at Him, and I didn't even know these kids. Why not be angry? They were in Mexico doing missionary work. How could God let them die? What kind of thanks is that? Of course, I just assumed that my sister would be angry, too. But she had a different perspective.

She said that they had all experienced a variety of feelings, but anger was not one of them. More than anything, Jaime said, there was an overwhelming sense of mercy and compassion that encircled them. They had come to Mexico to help several families build homes. Yet after the accident, it was the families they had come to help who comforted, supported and guided them. Roles reversed, and despite the sadness and grief experienced by all, love and compassion prevailed. As tragic as the accident was, God was able to teach the missionary students a valuable life lesson through the kindness of the Mexican families.

Frequently, though, when such tragedies happen, it is easier to blame God than try to understand what can be learned from the situation. It is important to know, however, that anger often is just a variable mask that guards our heart from the fear, confusion or sadness that is lingering in the midst. Sometimes it is simpler to get angry than to accept other such emotions that hurt so deeply. Eventually, though, it is important that we identify what we are actually feeling so that we can deal with those emotions and learn from our life experiences. Part of God's awesome humility is demonstrated when He accepts our misplaced anger and patiently waits for us to figure out what we are truly feeling.

Finally, when we stop being angry at God, we can open our hearts to His guidance, and with His help we can deal with our adversities. Like Amanda learned, when we lose perspective and become consumed with anger, sometimes it is essential to seek the guidance of someone who can give us a new outlook. In addition to God, Amanda's youth pastor helped her see her situation in a different light. Pastors, as well as parents, teachers, friends, counselors or any trusted adult, can provide objective guidance that may redirect our thoughts, lighten our load and give us a more positive attitude.

It is also essential to understand that, although it may be normal to blame God or become angry with Him, we should ask ourselves, "What kind of choice was made that led to this ultimate outcome?" For instance, perhaps someone chose to drink before they got behind the wheel of a car and as a result there was a fatal accident. This type of situation isn't God's fault; it is a human choice. Yet even if the fault lies with a specific individual, if we harden our hearts and become angry and unforgiving, the one we hurt the most is ourselves. I suppose we hurt God, too, because there is no room for love in anger and blame. God tells us in the Bible that without love, we are nothing. He says that love bears all things, believes all things, hopes all things and endures all things. I pray that in the future, when you feel angry, you will open your heart to God and let His love fill your soul.

AUTHOR'S NOTE: *If needed, please take time to turn to Appendix II at the end of the book for additional referral services for grief and loss, suicide, living with an addict and more.*

CHAPTER SEVEN

How Can You Forgive Me After What I Have Done?

Forgiveness
is an incredible gift . . .

The need to forgive and to be forgiven dwells within each of our hearts. Throughout this chapter, teens share experiences in which they looked for the Lord's forgiveness in their own lives or they sought God's strength to forgive someone else. If you identify with a particular story, I hope that it touches you with insight and direction. Forgiveness is an incredible gift from God, but it is also important to make choices every day that honor God in every way.

Mrs. T

God tells us to honor thy father and thy mother . . .

I fight with my mom all the time. If it's not about this, it's about that, and if it's not about that, it's about the other. People say we fight because we're alike and hearing that scares me. I had such a hard time growing up as battles between my mom and me escalated into World War III almost daily, especially when I was in high school. I knew that there was no way I'd survive if someone didn't change, and in my heart I doubted it would be my mom. The saying goes that you can't teach an old dog new tricks, and I was a younger dog, so I figured I'd have to be the one to change. But me change—HA! I'm perfect, or so I thought. So to do this and to really do it right, I had to dig deep—waaaaaaaaaaay deep.

God tells us to honor thy father and thy mother,

and through all of those tumultuous years, I wasn't honoring my mom. I even thought she was the one who was crazy. I began to pray, mostly because I didn't know what else to do, but also because a part of me knew that the only answer to the problem was in God. So I decided, or rather God helped me see, that I had to honor my mother. With honor, love is not automatic by any means; in fact, it isn't even required. But as I began to honor my mom, my love for her felt renewed. Also, honoring my mom brought me a great deal of peace. I mean peace in the sense of "no war," but peace also in the sense of tranquility. I think this feeling comes from God's forgiveness. When I finally looked to Him for guidance, I realized that I needed to ask His forgiveness for disrespecting my mom. For so long I thought it would always be a war with my mom, but God taught me otherwise. Believe me, there are still days when honoring my mother is the last thing on my mind. But even then, I remember the peace that God granted me through His forgiveness, and I am able to try just a little bit harder to be the daughter that He wants me to be.

Tawnie, 19

I was so blinded by the attention people were finally paying to me . . .

I was sixteen and a half. I had just finished my sophomore year of high school. It had been both a great academic year and a year of new experiences. I had passed my road test and received my driver's license. This was the greatest thing that had happened to me yet, but I never knew that having a car and gaining my independence would change my life. I had a very busy summer. I worked many hours and spent much time with my friends. At the beginning of junior year, however, my life changed. I believe that people knew me as a good kid who never got into trouble. Well, I was sick of being the angel of my class, so I made many poor decisions that year. One of these poor decisions was drinking.

I remember the first time that I drank, it was before a school dance and at the party everyone was shocked to see me with a beer in my hand. I was so blinded by the attention people were finally paying to me that I didn't realize that I was making a terrible mistake. This one incident was the catalyst to a chain reaction. People now started to notice me, and I became more popular with every beer I drank. This problem got so bad that all I could think about was drinking on the weekend. I didn't realize that I was getting into more trouble each weekend. I had become a whole other person, a person who I would have hated just a few months back.

As the year progressed, my problems worsened. I decided to try marijuana. I remember how terrible it was the first time, but that didn't stop me one bit! Just like drinking got out of control, so did drugs. Time passed, and now it was senior year. I was still drinking and smoking without a clue in the world. This drastically changed, however, when my parents found pot in my room. They were devastated to say the least. I sat through countless hours of discipline, and my heart shattered when my mom said, "We will never forgive you." When I heard this, I wanted to die. At this point, the only person I could really talk to was God. He was the only one who would listen to me. I was so depressed,

I didn't know what else to do but pray and ask God to help me through this most difficult time in my life. God forgave me when no one else would. I feel that I have matured now. I occasionally look back on my experiences last year and just a few months ago and realize I made a terrible mistake. I also think back on how God was there for me when I needed Him the most. He gives me the courage to live life the right way now and to make good decisions.

Patrick, 17

By dying on the cross,
He sets us free . . .

I had a friend, we were tight.
We stuck together, we'd never fight.

But then one day, her and I
We had a fight, over a guy.

I wasn't mad, but she was furious.
I asked her why, 'cuz I was curious.

She told me that she'd have to ponder,
If our friendship, could be any longer.

I talked to God, and asked him, "Please,
Can we be friends again, eventually?"

He didn't respond to me directly,
But in a way, He told me we could be.

For the next day, her face I did see.
She said, "I'm sorry, will you forgive me?"

God sets an example for us to see.
By dying on the cross, he sets us free.

My friend and I have learned to forgive.
For when God forgave, He showed us how to
    live.

                                        Kiran, 14

My regret was cheating...

Oh God, how can you forgive me? Some people regret having sex; others are ashamed of drinking. My regret was cheating. I always put pressure on myself to do well in school. One of my goals was to at least try to get good grades like my sister. As I learned, cheating definitely isn't the way to do it. I was in fifth grade. We would read a chapter or two in a book and then the teacher would give us a quiz based on questions. It wasn't like opinion-based essay questions either; the questions were more specific and needed an exact answer. They were very hard questions that would give me a weird feeling in the pit of my stomach because I didn't know all the answers. My friend and I sat at the same table. We decided that if we needed an answer, we would press on the other's toe and she would look off in space, and then you would sneak a peek at her paper. We did that one day and a girl behind us saw what we did and passed us a note that said, "I know you cheated, and I am going to tell the teacher." My mind started swirling, and my heart started beating rapidly.

The next day my friend and I told the teacher what we did, and she gave us a zero on that quiz. After going through about forty tissues and talking to my parents about it, I felt better, although the guilt seemed not to go away. I kept thinking, "What about God? Will He forgive me?" I started talking to Him nonstop. I learned my lesson after that terrible experience. I know that He forgave me because He has been helping me through a lot of tough stuff that I am going through right now. If you have ever regretted something you have done, talk to God because He will help you get over hard experiences and He will forgive you . . . just like He did me.

Erica, 15

... God is very patient ...

Most people want God to forgive them for things they regret they've done or for things they did wrong against His will or in His eyes. In my case, I want God to forgive me for the times when I've doubted Him and His choices for my life . . . for the times I thought I was right and He was wrong. God has a plan for all of us. He knows what is best for us. He's in control and He loves us. So, I think to myself, "How could I ever doubt such a fun-loving and forgiving God?"

If one of my friends were to doubt me, it would hurt my feelings. For example, if my best friend doubted that I could keep a secret, I would be crushed. I wonder if it hurts God's feelings when I doubt Him, too. Yet, He forgives me so easily. How does He do that? I think the answer is that God is very patient and He wants me to believe in Him. In which case, I definitely do!

Sometimes, though, people who believe in God have their doubts as well. I am so happy that God will still love us and forgive us when we doubt Him!

Carra, 14

This is when guilt comes in . . .

I've always wondered: What exactly is that little wave that goes over you when you've done something wrong? It starts in your brain and runs through your body, but mostly it dwells in your chest, near the middle but slightly to the left. Guilt—the pain you must live with or confess. It can stay with you for a second or last a lifetime, depending on what action you choose to take in response to it.

When I was about ten, I went to a store with my brother. He was about fourteen then. I was fascinated with all the various charms that they had to put on a necklace. Having this child's curiosity and no money, somehow the pretty trinkets found their way into my pocket. We left the store, went home and I looked over my new treasures. This is when guilt comes in. You know it is wrong, but either way you go, you lose because you've already made a poor choice in the first place. I think that the feeling of guilt may be God's way of helping you to do what is right. So the story ends by my parents finding out and making me take them back and apologize. Through my parents and my conscience, God showed me the right way and I will never steal anything again.

Valeri, 13

I've found the answer to all their problems and to mine: God! . . .

When I was a young teen, I started making some poor choices. I started out smoking pot, but that led to me using other drugs, and soon things got out of control and it seemed that I was ruining my life. Then, something happened in my life. I quit everything: all of the drugs and other bad choices I had made. I decided to pursue a relationship—a relationship like one I have never had. It was a relationship filled with unconditional love. I'm talking about a relationship with God. Everywhere I go and everything I hear from people these days is usually about all the problems they have or things that aren't going right for them. I've found the answer to all their problems and to mine: GOD! That's why I realized I was going nowhere. God had bigger and better plans for me. I can't tell you how nice it is just to know that I've always got somewhere to turn. Everything isn't perfect now, but it's a hundred times better than it was before. Through God's grace, I quit doing drugs. I quit drinking. I quit smoking. One thing I am not going to quit is this race. I'm going to stay in the battle, and I am fighting on the right side—God's.

Zacharia, 18

AUTHOR'S NOTE: *If you or someone you know is using alcohol or other drugs and would like to stop, you can call the National Referral Organization at 1-800-454-8966 for information on a treatment program near you.*

I finally realized that forgiveness is something to cherish . . .

I started going to church when my mom married my stepdad, and at the beginning I was unsure and felt out of place. But soon I became a Christian, and church and all that it entailed became a way of life. Everything was great. But not long after I was baptized, I began to feel like I was taking advantage of my religion. After I was told that God forgives you no matter what, I found myself doing things that I wouldn't normally do, only because I knew or I thought I knew at the time that I would be forgiven for it afterwards.

Someone once told me that you have a jar inside your soul for all of your sins. I think that if that were true, then the jar in my soul was overflowing, and something in my heart just clicked and I knew that I was doing the wrong *thing. I finally realized that forgiveness is something to cherish and not to take for granted. Now, I think hard before I do anything because I know that there will be consequences for my actions, even if I sincerely ask God to forgive me. It feels great to be truly sorry for what I have done in my past, but to be truly forgiven is even greater.*

Cherise, 14

I thought I was in love . . .

In the seventh grade, my best friend at the time was a strong Christian. She used to invite me to spend the night every Saturday, allowing me to go to church with her the next morning. I wasn't ever a person who went to church, but I began to like it more and more every time I went. Yet, at the same time, I was seeing a guy, and we were pretty serious. I thought I was in love with him and over the months, we chose to have sex a few times. As time went by, I began to become a regular at church and my relationship with my boyfriend ended. I knew then that I wasn't really in love.

A year later, I was saved and devoted my life to Christ. I felt so relieved and felt such a burden lifted from my shoulders when I turned my life over to God. It's been two years since I've been saved and became abstinent. No longer are my friend and I best friends. But, I thank God every day for her, because she led me down that path that brought Him into my life.

Tia, 16

I know that God forgives me . . .

God blessed me with a learning disability. Now, most people would say that a learning disability isn't a blessing, but I think it is. It is what makes me special. I didn't always feel that way, though. For a long time I was mad at God because of my disability. It was the hardest for me when I was in class, and the teacher would ask me to read out loud. I would just ask Him why He had to give it to me. Eventually, I learned that I shouldn't be mad at God because I have become such a stronger person because of my learning struggles. I know that God forgives me for being angry at Him. I also know that He gave this to me for a reason, and I accept it now, just like God accepts me!

Rebecca, 14

I partied all the time . . .

I was always searching for happiness but could never find it anywhere. Then I started to use drugs and drink. I thought, Hey, this is what it is all about. This is what I've been looking for. I really believed that happiness could be found with drinking and drugs. I partied all the time, and so did most of my friends. I ended up getting mixed up with the wrong group of people. I mean, I am a smart person and I always did well in school. But, all of a sudden all I could do was look at a blank page and know that it was due the next day and that I had five more to write after the first one. That's what partying did to me. Nothing was more important. I began to think that there was always time for school, but partying was in the here and now. I got by, barely.

Things just kept getting harder. People started

to move on and get over the party scene, but I couldn't seem to. Then somebody took me to a Bible study. I started to build a relationship with God. Life started again! I could actually remember what I did two days ago and who I was calling on the telephone. God did something for me that the drinking and drugs didn't do. He gave me that peace that I was always looking for. I always thought I was happy before and that I had real friends, but once I stopped partying I really found out who my friends were. It's all right; I know now that I always will have somebody to turn to. Even though I can't see God, I know that He is there listening to everything I have to say. It's funny, I wasted five years of my life partying. Now, I feel like I can still be somebody and go somewhere, but I know I can't do it alone.

Jorge, 19

AUTHOR'S NOTE: *If you'd like to seek help for a drug or alcohol problem, I encourage you to call 1-800-454-8966 for a referral for treatment.*

. . . *I got jealous*

Do you know how it feels to be sorry, but not forgiven? I do. My friend, Jodi, and I were very close. We always went to the movies together, and we were inseparable. She told me her deepest secrets, and I told her mine. She told me about every boy she liked, and I swore not to tell.

When we were in the eighth grade, we loved to talk about guys. Jodi told me that she really liked this new boy at school named Scott. One day at lunch, we got into an argument because she was spending the weekend with someone other than me, and I got jealous. I was so mad that I made the mistake of telling Scott that Jodi liked him. Jodi found out, and she was so hurt and mad at me. I felt terrible. That night I cried and cried, and then I noticed I wasn't hoping so much for Jodi's forgiveness; I was praying for God's. I realized that although Jodi's forgiveness would have helped, God's forgiveness was what I truly needed. Because when I broke the promise I made to Jodi, I also broke the promise I made to God to be honest and true. Jodi did forgive me, and all it took on my part was for me to tell her I was sorry. More importantly, though, that is all it took for God to forgive me, too!

Alisha, 15

"J" Talk

The story that I am about to share with you is very serious and exceptionally sad. But I have chosen to share it because I believe that within this powerful story, a valuable lesson can be learned.

Courtney was only fourteen and extremely drunk on the summer night that she was raped. Her rapist was someone she considered a friend. She trusted him, and he betrayed that trust. Sadly, Courtney feels that she betrayed herself, as well. She knows that the rape was not her fault, but she blames herself for choosing to get drunk. In fact, Courtney was so drunk that when this guy, who was nineteen, asked her to come back to his room so he could show her something, she went with him, trailing her hands along the wall to maintain her balance. Once there, she began to feel sick. He told her to lie down on his bed and that he would stay with her and protect her. Apparently, Courtney passed out. The next thing she remembered, she felt like she was being shaken. It was only then that she realized that she was being forced to have sex. Courtney struggled as she screamed, hoping that her friends down the hall would hear her. She pleaded and begged him to stop, and finally he did, saying, "I was finished with you anyway." When he walked away, he took Courtney's virginity with him.

Courtney cried as she told me her story. She felt worthless, dirty and guilty. "How could somebody do that?" she asked. How could she let herself get into that situation? Courtney kept the rape a secret for almost two months, as her dignity and self-confidence disintegrated. Finally, no longer able to hide from the truth, Courtney confessed the rape to her parents and the authorities so that he would not go unpunished.

Still, Courtney carried a heavy burden on her shoulders. She felt an intense emptiness inside and began to shut everyone out. Even her mom, who was there for Courtney in every way, could not fill the void that was growing in her heart. Her mom told her, "It's going to be okay, Courtney. I'm here for you." But Courtney didn't feel it would be okay. She didn't understand how she could ever overcome her feelings of hopelessness. Many people, myself included, pleaded with Courtney not to blame herself. I specifically told Courtney that it is never the fault of the victim for being raped. If a person does not give consent, resists or says "no" and is forced to have sex, it is rape and only the assailant can take the blame. Yet, when she thought about the party scene that she had become involved in over the summer, she was afraid that she had disappointed God.

Courtney remembers a particular night when she threw herself across her bed sobbing and pleading with God. Tears streaked her face as she prayed, "God, please don't let me wake up in the morning." Immediately, she felt at peace. Not because she thought God would grant her prayer; in fact, she knew the opposite was occurring. Courtney said that as she lay on her bed, she sensed God's presence. She felt as if He physically wrapped His arms around her, and she began to feel whole again. Courtney experienced an unwavering conviction that she was still accepted by God and that with His forgiveness and help she would get through her ordeal.

God's grace is abundant. His mercy abounds. Teens often assume that God will turn His back on them if they make a poor choice or do something they regret. Maybe they think this way because they have experienced this type of reaction from their friends. It is not uncommon for friends to, at least temporarily, turn against each other if they have been hurt or disappointed. For example, if a close friend betrays your confidence, even after you make up, you may harbor hurt or anger toward that person. Although you love your friend, there may be a small part of you that can never forgive his or her disloyalty. Fortunately, God's love is much bigger than our love. When God forgives you, He forgives forever. He never brings it back and throws it in your face. When He forgives, He is able to forget, too.

My friend Janell uses a fantastic analogy to demonstrate God's grace and forgiveness. She tells the story of an experience she encountered at a Christian retreat. She awoke early one morning and decided she needed some quiet time. With a cup of tea in hand, she walked down to a river. As she stood by the river, she began to contemplate all of the wonderful Christians at this retreat. Compared to them she felt unworthy. As she prayed, she pondered the mistakes she had made in her life, all of her failures and sins, and she found herself staring down at her cup of tea. Brown in color, the tea looked dirty and stagnant. Janell felt much the same way. Then she looked at the river. It was running gloriously clear, clean and beautiful. In what she believes was an answer to prayer, Janell felt God encouraging her to throw her tea into the river. It was as if He was saying, "Give me your worries and your troubles. Give me your regrets and faults, and I will sweep them away in this river. Never will they come back. Your life can flow clear and clean now, no longer dirty or stagnant." As Janell emptied the contents of her cup into the river, she noticed that her tea didn't taint the beautiful rushing water and, in that moment, she felt refreshed, renewed and worthy.

Like Janell, there may be times in your life when you feel undeserving of God's love. Teenagers frequently make choices that they later regret. Sometimes it is difficult for teens to think beyond the moment. When you're at a party and everyone is drinking and seeming to have fun, it is easy to rationalize drinking yourself. But when I speak to youth groups, I always tell teens that drinking and God don't mix. Not only does God use the Bible to tell us that drunkenness is a sin, but think about it: When you drink, you lose your ability to make sound decisions. Even if you set limits for your drinking, those boundaries are often broken. It is more common for one drink to turn into five than for a teen to stop at just one.

Many teens who choose to use drugs or have sex for the first time do so *after* they have been drinking. I have spoken with teenagers who regret having lost their virginity after a night of partying. They want to take it back, but they can't. They are worried about sexually transmitted diseases and pregnancy. But they hadn't thought about it at the time, because under the influence of alcohol, they had lost their sense of good judgment. Rape, too, is a risk. Courtney said that had she been thinking clearly, she wouldn't have gone alone into a bedroom with a guy who was five years older than her. Nor would she have passed out, leaving him the opportunity to violate her.

Also, the use of drugs and alcohol among teens is not only illegal with consequences of arrest, but teenagers who drink and drug also risk their lives. Many studies indicate that the leading cause of teen death is accidents, and the majority of these are related to substance abuse. Remember Brandy's story at the beginning of this book? Finally, teens who choose to use drugs or alcohol jeopardize their freedom. I'm not referring to jail time, although that can be a realistic result. I am talking about addiction.

If you use drugs or alcohol habitually, you risk addiction and can become a prisoner of your need. Scripture teaches that your physical body is the temple of the Holy Spirit. How can you serve God and addiction, too?

It is also important to understand that when considering your physical body as the temple of the Holy Spirit, in addition to abstaining from drugs and alcohol, it is spiritually right to be abstinent from sex before marriage. I have read several references to a study that indicated half of all teens surveyed were sexually active or had been at some point in their teen years. That tells me two things. First, if you are a virgin, praise God! Know that you are not alone— 50 percent of your peers value their virginity, too. Second, there are teenagers out there who are making a choice to be sexually active. But I already knew this from speaking with my students or kids in youth groups. The choice for teens to be sexually active can be a matter of curiosity, acceptance or temptation. Yet, regardless of a person's reason, the Bible has something to say about it.

God speaks often in the Bible of sexual immorality as a sin. Also, God calls us to save ourselves for the person that we marry. The Bible tells us to refrain from sex until marriage because sexual intercourse is a sacred and intimate act that should only be shared within the union of husband and wife. Within the sanctity of marriage, sexual intimacy can be a wonderful experience and a blessing. God didn't say, "Sex is bad!" In fact, He created sex. Don't forget, though, He also gave us boundaries for sexual behavior. I encourage you to save sex for marriage. Offer it to your husband or wife on your wedding night as a precious gift that you have treasured and withheld to share with the person with whom you want to spend the rest of your life.

I have had many teens ask me, "How can I rate with God after what I've done?" Regardless of the choice that a teen may have made to lead to his or her need for forgiveness, God lays out the answer for us plainly. The Bible proclaims that if we feel sorry for what we have done and we sincerely ask God to forgive us, He will. God lifts the burden of sin from our hearts and grants us His mercy. Like the free-flowing river, God doesn't recycle past sins. When He forgives, He forgives forever and His grace overflows.

AUTHOR'S NOTE: *I realize that Courtney's story is very tragic and I pray that you never experience such an ordeal. However, I feel compelled to give you the following information as a resource: Rape, Abuse and Incest National Network (RAINN), 1-800-656-4673.*

CHAPTER EIGHT

Hey God, Can You Hear Me Way Up There?

I pray that you will take from their testimonies . . .

"Hey God, Can You Hear Me Way Up There?" I chose this chapter title because I know that some teens feel as if God is "too far away" to actually talk to. However, when you read passages from this chapter, I believe that you will see how close prayer can actually bring you to God. Teens share their stories and their philosophies of prayer. I pray that you will take from their testimonies a notion of the peace, comfort, strength and hope that can be found in having a conversation with the Lord.

Mrs. T

I tell God about my plans . . .

I have not been to church in over four years;
every selfish Sunday, I sleep in until the sun is so
bright that I can sleep no longer. I do, however,
pray every day. At night, when I have gotten off
the phone from talking to my friends or my
boyfriend, I turn off all the lights, get into bed
and have a nice talk with God. I tell God all
about my day, what I enjoyed and what upset
me. I tell God about my plans for the next day,
and that I hope He protects me while I sleep. I
always thank God for giving me such wonderful
people in my life. I thank Him for allowing me to
be a healthy, happy, intelligent sixteen-year-old
girl whose biggest worry is what I am going to
wear the next day or if I did all of my homework.
I like to pray for all the people in the world who
are scared, sick, cold, hungry or hurting in any
way.

Talking to God each night makes me feel incredibly blessed and lucky for the life the Lord has given me. When I take time to reflect on my day by talking to God, it makes me happy to be alive. The Lord makes my daily problems and frustrations feel very insignificant compared to the love He has shown me. Since I was very young, I have seen God as an open journal. Each night I record my feelings and thoughts. He reads them over and guides me on what to do. God is always listening. God is your oldest and best friend. He knows everything about you and does not judge you. Talking to God every day is very good for letting go of stress. It helps me to relax and feel at peace. I fall asleep knowing that I am loved by Him and that all of His children are here for a reason. Never be afraid to tell God anything—He already knows what you are going to say. The Lord is a patient friend when you feel you have no one.

Kinzie, 16

That's why I love praying . . .

Friendships come and friendships go. I often don't know who is on my side. Some days I feel like everything is going my way; I will be laughing with my friends and just having fun. But then other days, I hear the rumors and gossip that are part of every high-school life and I don't know what to believe. The person I thought was my best friend the day before all of a sudden seems distant to me. I feel alone and confused. I turn to God. I try to pray to God at night after a rough day. I tell Him what's bothering me and get everything off my chest. I often feel better just from letting all of my pent-up feelings out and knowing somebody is listening. Having faith gives me the courage to deal with everyday struggles I go through, and knowing someone is always listening makes me feel a little better. That's why I love praying to God.

Sandra, 17

I pray in my own way . . .

My mother often tells me to pray when I have a problem, but I don't really pray; I just sort of reflect upon my life. I pray in my own way, in my own time. I don't really believe it's fair to sit there and pray to God only when you need His help. It seems like you should be more devoted. Another way I pray is that I say my prayers every night before bed. I don't say them to gain recognition or even when I do something terrible; I just say them because it's my little way of saying "hi" to God so that He knows that I am here, and I am enjoying knowing that He is watching over me.

Joanna, 18

I might not have gotten what I prayed for, but I get . . .

I have never been a very prayerful person. In fact, I am not even particularly religious. But what is really great is that it doesn't matter. Every time I have really prayed, prayed from my soul, God was always there. Whenever I needed Him most, He has always helped me. When I pray a really general prayer for help or guidance, He always listens. A prayer coming from me, the one who is not religious or formal or anything, still reaches God and He still listens. My prayers that I really need are usually answered. Something will guide or help me in some way. Even when my prayers seem unanswered, God is still there watching out for me. I might not have gotten what I prayed for, but I got what I needed. And then it makes me wonder. Was I praying for the right thing? Did I really *want or need that? And is what actually happened better anyway? So the next time you are down or in a jam, give God a ring. He will be there for you, and you don't even have to pay long-distance charges.*

Daniel, 18

When I pray, I start off by . . .

When life isn't going so great, I have a strong urge to talk to Jesus. I stop what I am doing and get down to praying. I pray because Jesus is the most important thing in my life, and just knowing that He died for my sins and is always with me makes me want to pray to Him. When I pray, I start off by admitting that I am a sinner. I ask Him to forgive me for what I have done. I tell Him that I am blessed that He is there to forgive me. I tell Him that I love Him, and that His love and glory will never leave my soul. I trust in Him, and I know that He will never abandon me. When I am done pouring my heart out to God, I tell Him what's on my mind or I sing praises to Him, or I just let Him know that I am happy that He is in my life. Praying is such a large part of my life. My spirit is lifted when I pray. The Lord has blessed me in so many ways,

I feel guilty about all the sins that I have committed. Although God lifts this guilt from my heart when He forgives me, I then pray that I will make better decisions in the future.

Callie, 14

I used to think we could only talk to God in church . . .

God is available at any time. God is always
around for us. I have talked to Him many times
in prayer. I used to think we could only talk to
God in church or before we go to bed. But now,
I have learned we can pray to God anytime, and
He will listen. I am very forgetful and often find
myself in nerve-racking situations. When I lose
my keys, wallet or something important, I say a
quick prayer to God asking for help to find my
missing thing. Soon after, I'll suddenly stumble
upon it or remember where I left it. After kicking
myself for not seeing or remembering the lost
object and its location, I say a quick thank-you
prayer and move on. I also pray on nights when
I am up very late trying to get a report done for
the next day. I ask for help to finish and for
enough strength in the next morning to get by. I

will also talk to God when I am opening at work, and it's very dark out and the buildings look scary. I'll just talk to God, and having someone to talk to makes me feel better. God is around in other situations, as well. I prayed to Him after hearing a friend was thinking of committing suicide, when my parents were sick and many other times when I couldn't get by alone.

Why not turn to friends? Friends aren't always home, and they don't always have the answers. God might not give you the exact answer, but He will push you in the right direction. God is around for us 24/7. He is never off at a party or soccer game. He is where we need Him the most. I don't think of prayer as a "church thing" where you have to recite old lines from younger days, but as a conversation with a friend who never fades. I feel comfortable with this because He always answers in some way and never ignores me.

LaTania, 17

Some of God's greatest gifts are the unanswered prayers . . .

If you are doubting God because of an unanswered prayer and don't know where you stand in your faith journey, then this simple lesson that I learned may speak to your heart and hopefully answer your questions, especially if your question is the one that most kids ask themselves: "Why doesn't He answer my prayers?"

The lesson is this: Some of God's greatest gifts are the unanswered prayers. God has His reasons for what He answers and what He doesn't. Either way, though, He's still there and loves you more than anything.

Allison, 14

I feel I can say anything to Him . . .

I pray to God because I feel when I talk to Him, He truly listens. I feel I can say anything to Him and He will understand. I pray to God because some things I am just not comfortable saying in front of others. So I say them to God because I know that He is always listening and will always understand what I am going through.

Nathan, 14

I've lived with my grandparents for ten years . . .

I never used to pray for help from God as much as I should have, but since this recent court case with my mom and dad, I've learned to pray as much as I can. This is why:

I've lived with my grandparents for ten years, and I feel like they're my parents now. My mom and dad want to take that away from me, and they don't understand how I feel or what I want. They actually don't care about what I want or feel. They only care about themselves. The reason that I started to live with my grandparents in the first place is because my mom and dad weren't married, they were both drug users, and my dad was violent and he beat my mom and all of his other girlfriends. My mom and I had to go to a battered women's shelter. My grandma offered to take me for a while until my mom got her stuff together. My mom agreed, and a little while turned into seven

*years. During this time, my grandparents got cus-
tody of me. I was glad because I didn't want to go
back to my mom or my dad.*

*A little while after I was going to turn twelve,
my mom and dad took me and my grandparents
to court. So before the day of court, I prayed my
heart out that I could stay with my grandparents. I knew that my grandparents and me
would need God's courage to get through this
battle, so I prayed for that, too. The day of court,
my mom and dad both lied. They said that they
weren't on drugs, which they were, and my dad
said that he wasn't violent. My mom also said
that my grandparents stole me from her, which
was completely untrue. So after court, I prayed
that everything was going to be all right.*

*Now, I know that sometimes when you pray, it
doesn't always work out like you want, but when
we went back to court to hear the judge's decision, I was amazed that we got what we wanted
and more. My mom and dad made some bad
choices, and it finally caught up with them. The
judge saw through it, and so did I. Right now, I
love my mom and dad, but I will never live with
them or be as close to them as I am with my real
parents—my grandma and grandpa!*

Lauren, 12

AUTHOR'S NOTE: *If you are able to identify with Lauren's situation because you live in the presence of addiction and/or abuse, please seek help. The following resources can lead you to support services in your area: National Youth Crisis Hotline: 1-800-HIT-HOME (1-800-448-4663); National Resource Center on Domestic Violence: 1-800-537-2238.*

You don't have to make an appointment with Him . . .

When I pray to God, I pray for help. I find a quiet place where I can be alone and concentrate. God is always there. You don't have to make an appointment with Him or call Him up; you just think. I don't even need to say it out loud; I just think to myself what I want Him to hear. It feels good to know that He is always there.

Rebecca, 14

Does He still listen to my prayers?

I often think, Is God still protecting my soul? Does He still listen to my prayers? Does He still feel my pain? Or, does He look down on me for the choices that I have made in my life? *But when I pray at night, I let God know that I am sorry for the sins I have committed, but there is nothing I or God can do to change those decisions. If someone were to ask me if I am ashamed of ever doing drugs, I would say "no," because now that I am off drugs, I feel that I am stronger in a way.*

Remember this: There is no way to change the bad decisions we make in life, but we can learn from our mistakes and make better choices in the future. By doing this, it makes us stronger. So, do I think God still listens to my prayers or shares my pain? Yes, I do, because I feel that no matter what kind of choices I make, God is still with me to help me and to show me a better way. God won't make us do the right thing. All He can do is show us the path to follow. It is our choice to actually follow that path.

Curt, 16

My favorite aunt died of AIDS . . .

My favorite aunt died of AIDS when I was about sixteen years old. For the first week, I blamed God. I asked Him how He could do this to me. I was hurt and didn't know who to blame. After the first week, I realized that I didn't need someone to blame. I needed someone to talk to so I could stay sane. One night, I finally turned to the one who has always heard me out. I apologized because I realized that He didn't take her from me. She would always be in my heart, in my memories and in my prayers. He took her from the pain. Not many people believe me, but that night after my prayer, I felt a presence in my room with me, right there on my bed. I believe that God sent me my auntie as an angel for that moment so that I could say good-bye. He knew that was all I needed to stop my tears. I asked Him for it in my prayer. I know what I felt.

I know whose presence it was, and I know whom to thank. I finally slept for the first time in a week. Thank you again, God.

Rosa, 18

I pray when I am on the go . . .

I pray for two reasons: one is to ask God for something, and the other is to thank Him. He is all-powerful. I pray when I am on the go. I'll have something to pray about, and I'll stop for a minute and think of God. I may petition, or I may thank Him. But then I am back on my way feeling that God is with me. In asking for something, I never try to test God. I trust that He is all-knowing and that the answer to my prayers is the answer that I need. So I pray open-minded prayers. My favorite prayer, the one most meaningful to me, is, "God, Thy will be done." It reminds me that God is in control, so whatever happens is His will, out of His goodness, grace and understanding. And sometimes things don't go exactly as I would like them to, but I know that though I may not understand why, God does, and I have to trust His answers.

Phillip, 17

*I prayed for God
to comfort my friend . . .*

Recently, my best friend's father passed away. He died of a terminal illness that he had been fighting for years. Every time he grew worse, he would set goals for how long he wanted to live. If it was near Christmas, he would pray for the strength to survive past Christmas or other important times, so that his family wouldn't have to think of that holiday as a sad time. The last few weeks of his life were the worst for him because he was in so much pain, and it was the hardest on my friend because she had to watch her father go through this.

Watching how my friend would put on a happy face for others when she would later come to me crying was the hardest thing ever. I knew how unhappy she was, and I did everything I could in my power to comfort her. I would listen anytime she needed to talk, no matter the time, and I would give her my shoulder when she needed to cry. We would discuss how she was feeling, how her father was doing or how her mother was taking it. My friend told me how her father wasn't who he used to be, not by choice, but because of the medication he was taking. One night, after getting off the phone with my friend, I knelt at my bed and prayed. I prayed for God to comfort my friend and her mother, and to take her father's pain away. I couldn't handle how hurt my friend was and how much pain her father was in. I wanted his pain to go away more than anything in the world, and I knelt there in the dark, alone, praying to God to help my friend in her time of need. Afterwards, I climbed into bed and fell fast asleep.

The next morning, my mother woke me to inform me that my friend's father had passed away last night. I was completely devastated and sad. After I cried tears for all that their family had been through, I called my friend to see how she was. She said she was sad, but also glad because now her father's pain was over and he was in heaven, smiling down upon her and her mother.

Linna, 16

. . . God is there to talk to always

I used to pray every night before I went to bed. It was something that I was taught to do. Mom said that there was something about having your hands in such a position that would reach God so He could know you had something to say to Him. So, I did this. When I was a little girl, my prayers were just an ordinary routine, "Now I lay me down to sleep, I pray the Lord my soul to keep . . ." and so on. When I was younger, I don't think my prayers meant much. I said them to make God proud of me for saying them. As I grew up, my prayers changed. They slowly grew to mean more and more. But then I stopped praying for a while, until about five months ago. That is when I found out that my grandma had cancer, and since then I've never prayed so much in my life.

When I first found out, flashes of memory came back to me of when I was ten and my grandpa died of cancer. I knew what was next for my grandma, and I didn't like it. My grandpa's death was the hardest thing I've ever had to deal with since I've been alive. After Grandpa died of cancer, my routine praying stopped. In fact, I rarely ever prayed. I know it's wrong, but I got so mad at God for taking some-one so special from me, especially after all the times I prayed to Him asking Him not to take my grandpa away from me. I figured, God must not be listening to me in my prayers. I had no desire to talk to God after that . . . until I heard about Grandma.

Once I found out that Grandma had cancer and only had a 50 percent chance of it being removed, I realized there was no way that I could get through this alone. I needed help. My grandma is one of the most important people in my life. When my mom got off the phone and told me through thick tears that Grandma had cancer, I exploded. I remember punching my fists into the walls and screaming "No!" All thoughts of my grandpa dying of cancer raced through my mind. This can't happen to Grandma, too. How could God do this? I had to ask Him. The only way I was taught to talk to God was through recited prayers. The difference now was I found myself always praying for my grandma, with any words I could find in my heart. I would pray while I was on the phone, in class, during my softball games, everywhere. I also found that you don't have to fold your hands to reach up and talk to God. In fact, you don't even have to move your lips. I prayed all of the time.

Grandma went into surgery, and a few days later, the results of the procedure were given to us. When I heard the cancer had been completely removed, I cried almost as hard as I did when I found out she had it. I was so relieved, and the hurt inside started to leave me. It's such a great feeling. I thank God for this because I know He had everything to do with it. I know now, looking back on those days when I didn't pray, that it wasn't right for me to be angry at Him. My grandpa is gone now, and that is something I have to live with every day of my life. But, I know now that everything happens for a reason. Even though God didn't make my grandparents have cancer, I learned from both situations. I also know now that God is there to talk to always. Even if it seems like He's not listening, He is. He listens to everyone.

Sabrina, 14

*. . . my dad held my hands
and we prayed . . .*

"If you just can't take it, take it to the Lord."
That would make a great magnet. Although it
may seem cheesy . . . it's true. Sometimes when I
feel like life is weighing me down, I pray. I take
it to the Lord. To me, prayer is just like talking to
my father. You don't need to be anyone special
to talk to God. In fact, He wants you to talk to
Him. When I pray, I feel like a burden has been
lifted from my shoulders.

One of the many prayers God has answered for
me is when He delivered my mom from drugs.
She wasn't into them heavily, but just enough to
break our family apart. Ever since I could
remember, my parents would be fighting or my
mom would move out for a while and stay with
her friends. When this would happen, my dad,
whom I admire very much, wouldn't get all

worked up and yell; he would pray. As a matter of fact, I can remember an instance when we were standing in the kitchen and my dad held my hands and we prayed that my mom would realize sooner rather than later that she couldn't live without God in her life. That was seven years ago, and we are only now beginning to see the benefit of our prayers. So, when you talk to God, you need to be patient. Results don't often happen overnight. And even when prayers are answered, we still need to pray to God and thank Him for everything.

Olivia, 14

AUTHOR'S NOTE: *If someone in your family has a problem with alcohol, I encourage you to call Al-Anon/Alateen at 1-800-356-9996. They can refer you to support services for family members of addicts.*

Some things I ask Him don't come true, but I keep believing . . .

Sometimes I ask God things, like please let me win my soccer game or please make the guy I have a crush on go out with me. I know these are simple things, but I ask anyway, because I just feel like it's okay with God. Some things I ask Him don't get answered, but I keep believing because life would be too easy if everything you wanted just happened. Also, if He doesn't answer one of my prayers, I have to think of all He has given me: love, family, friends, freedom, happiness and everything I need to live. God is a friend when I need one, a source of hope when I have none, and someone I trust with all my heart.

Rachelle, 15

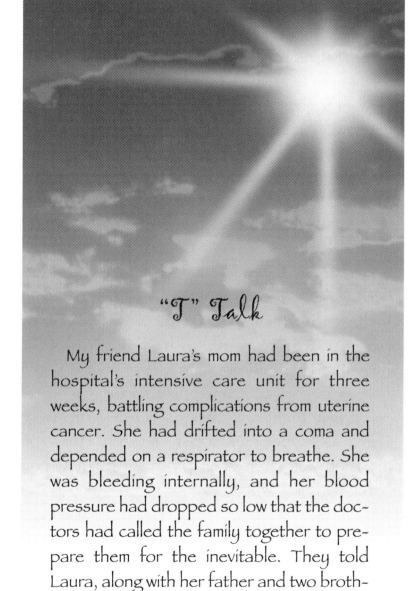

"T" Talk

My friend Laura's mom had been in the hospital's intensive care unit for three weeks, battling complications from uterine cancer. She had drifted into a coma and depended on a respirator to breathe. She was bleeding internally, and her blood pressure had dropped so low that the doctors had called the family together to prepare them for the inevitable. They told Laura, along with her father and two brothers, that they didn't expect her mother to make it through the night. If the family wanted to say good-bye, they'd better do it quickly. At that point, there was no hope for recovery. Laura and her family went directly to her mom's room. Laura remembers telling her mother, "Mom, if you want to fight to live, now is the time. You have to do it now!" Yet, on the way home to get blankets and pillows to take back to the hospital so that they could stay by her mom's side on what would surely be her last night, Laura's conviction that her mom could fight to live deteriorated into hopelessness and desperation.

Once home, Laura left her dad sobbing on the couch while she went upstairs to gather bedding. On the way upstairs, she took a promise book full of prayers and scripture verses from the bookshelf. She entered her bedroom and then crumbled to the floor as desperate tears poured from her eyes. Feeling distraught and alone, she prayed to God. "This is all happening too fast," she told Him. "You haven't answered one of my prayers. God, have you abandoned me? Where are you?" And then Laura says that as she lay on the floor, hysterically sobbing, she begged God, "Lord, please give me something. If you are going to take my mother, give me something to let me know that you are real, that you can hear me. Give me something that will bring me comfort in this pain."

At that point, Laura opened her promise book to a random page, and the words leapt off the paper and filled her heart with peace. For they said, "Believe in me and do not doubt, for I am here. I am with you. Trust me." Laura said that the instant she read those words, she knew deep inside her heart that not only had God given her comfort, He also answered her prayer with a feeling of absolute assurance that her mom would be okay. She said that all the fear and hopelessness that she had felt when she came upstairs extraordinarily vanished into an overwhelming sense of calm. In fact, Laura said she felt bathed in peace.

Laura went directly downstairs and hugged her heartbroken father. "Dad," she said. "Mom will be okay." Laura's brothers pulled her aside and asked her not to make this harder on their father. They were sure that Laura's hope was desperate and futile. But Laura didn't let them discourage her. The Holy Spirit had touched her heart. God had answered her prayer. Laura believed like she had never believed before.

They had only been gone an hour when they arrived back at the hospital. Laura's dad had stopped to talk with someone in the lobby, while Laura went to her mom's room. Miraculously, but of no surprise to Laura, her mother's blood pressure was up, her need for extra oxygen was down and her condition was stabilizing. Laura ran down the hall to tell her father. She exclaimed, "Dad, you are not going to believe this!" In fact, he didn't. Knowing that he had to prepare his daughter, he told her that he knew she felt hopeful, but they still had to anticipate the unavoidable fact that her mother would die. But Laura knew that her mom would live. And she did! In the days to follow, they were able to take her mom off the respirator as she came out of her coma and began to breathe on her own. The first time that Laura's mom spoke after they removed the respirator, she confided, "I saw God's face the whole time I was asleep."

Prayer is an awesome concept. Can we really talk to God? Does He actually listen? Can He truly answer? I know that many teens, as well as adults, struggle with the immensity of prayer. But I believe that the answer to all of these questions is a resounding "YES!" We can talk to God. He does hear because He cares about each and every one of us. And, He does answer our prayers. However, I didn't always feel so confident about prayer.

I actually used to believe that you had to be especially worthy in order for prayer to really work. I even remember listening to the leaders of my high-school youth group pray out loud and thinking, "I'll never be able to pray that well." I thought that my prayers had to be as eloquent and organized as theirs were. What I later learned, though, was that as long as your prayer is sincere, *how* a person prays doesn't matter to God. Well-articulated prayers are not on God's priority list. God cares what your heart is saying, not your lips.

I have spoken with many teens who say that the reason they don't pray is because they don't know how. Well, if you know how to carry on a conversation with a friend, then you can pray to God. Talk to Him. Tell Him about your day. Share with Him your worries. If you are feeling bad about something, admit that to Him, too. It will make you feel so much better inside, just to know that God knows you're sorry for what you have done. It will also allow Him an opportunity to grant you forgiveness. The Lord wants this type of relationship with you. He wants you to feel comfortable talking to Him. God also wants to answer your prayers.

It is true that some people hear God actually speak to them, but most do not. Usually, God speaks to us subtly. Sometimes, He gives us a feeling. Often God uses self-reflection as a means to answer prayer. When we listen to our own conscience, God provides endless and steadfast responses to our prayers. While other times, He presents us with a circumstance or situation that guides our path. However, it is up to us to recognize His guidance and acknowledge His answers. Sometimes I think that God puts an answer right in front of our noses, but because it is not exactly what we expected or specifically what we asked for, we don't recognize it.

This reminds me of a story I once heard about a man who was standing on the roof of his house during a flood. The water was rising higher and moving faster. In fact, it was almost up to the edge of the roof. The man prayed to God and asked God to rescue him. A few moments later, a couple in a small rowboat came by. They said to the man, "Get in, we will take you to safety." The man said, "Don't worry about me; God will save me." The water got even higher and a larger rescue boat came to save the man. He sent them away, telling them that he was counting on God to rescue him. Soon the man felt water swirling around his ankles. It moved quickly up his legs to his waist. A helicopter appeared and rescuers begged the man to grab the rope that they threw down to him. The man, with much conviction in his voice, yelled up to the chopper, "No, go save someone else. I prayed to God. I know that He will save me!" Moments later, the man was washed away by the water and he drowned in the flood. When he got to heaven, he asked God, "Lord, why didn't you answer my prayer and rescue me?" God looked at the man with a wry grin on His face and said, "I did! I sent you a rowboat, a rescue boat and a helicopter!"

You see the man didn't recognize God's answer because he was blinded by his own expectations. Having faith that God will answer our prayers doesn't mean slacking off and just waiting for God to provide. Sometimes, I think that prayer, or even God for that matter, can be used as an excuse. For example, if you pray to God for a good after-school job and then every day you go home after school, eat ice cream and watch TV while you wait for God to drop a job in your lap, it just isn't going to happen. I actually believe that God expects more from us than that. He gave each of us talents and abilities. He encourages us to take initiative. His answers aren't always obvious or immediate. Sometimes we learn lessons while we wait. That, in itself, is a gift from God.

At the same time, occasionally His answer occurs in an *unanswered* prayer. For example, you may pray with intensity about getting together with a particular guy or girl whom you have been in love with forever. Yet, your prayer may go unanswered. This doesn't happen because God wants to see you sad or deprived. It is more likely that He knows this

person isn't right for you. God can see a bigger picture than we can. He can see what lies ahead of us,
while we are limited by our needs of the moment.
This may also explain why sometimes miracles occur,
while other times they don't. My friend Laura's
answered prayer was an obvious miracle. However, I
know many people who have prayed intensely for a
miracle, yet nothing happens. Sometimes we just
have to trust that God knows what is best for us.
Likely, what appears to be an unanswered prayer to
us is actually answered as "wait" or "no" from God.

Perhaps you are reading this and you've never
prayed before. You can start by letting your first
prayer be one that establishes a relationship with
God. Ask Him to enter your heart and fill you with
His Spirit. He wants that more than anything. I was
speaking with a girl once who told me that it made
her uncomfortable to pray. The more we talked
about it, the more she realized that although she
was trying to talk to God, she didn't have a personal
relationship with Him. It would be like trying to start
up an intimate conversation with a stranger in an ele-
vator. You will be hindered by the boundaries of
your remoteness.

Yet if you open your heart to the Lord, I think
you'll find that He is pretty easy to talk to. You will
also discover that prayer is very rewarding. Sharing

our worries and fears, as well as our triumphs and praises with God, is like confiding in a best friend. Like Kinzie suggests in her excerpt, God is the one person that she tells everything to, because He is always listening and understanding, for He knows her heart like no one else. Kinzie also knows that the answers to her life problems often reside within the power of God's love. My friend Laura learned this, too.

Today, Laura's mom has been in remission for over five years. Laura has told me that the spiritual experience that she encountered on the eve of her mother's recovery has taught her so much. Mostly, she realized that sometimes you have to let your whole being and soul be laid down before God. Prior to her prayer of desperation, Laura had put conditions on her prayers. She had tried to stay in control and she told God what she thought should happen, rather than surrendering her problems to Him. She said that she would pray often, but she never turned her mother's sickness and situation completely over to God. Laura would give the Lord her worries, but then quickly grab them back and let them gnaw at her heart, while they grew bigger and bigger. Now, she prays for the presence of mind and heart to truly let go and completely submit her concerns to God.

Laura also learned that answered prayers come in many forms. God touched Laura's heart and gave her reassurance in an overwhelming feeling of peace. He also guided her to the faithful words in her promise book that gave her the comfort and hope she had been lacking. Let Laura's lessons be guidance for you as well. Know that God gave us prayer as a means to communicate with Him. Prayer is His gift to you. Make use of it and feel the power of God's love and guidance work in your life.

CHAPTER NINE

I Love You, Lord!

. . . a fresh discovery of God's love . . .

This chapter will fill your heart with joy as you read passages from teens who share how their love for the Lord has filled their lives. Through their perspectives, you will also be taken on a journey that will lead to a fresh discovery of God's love in your life. I believe that all people can benefit from renewing their spirit in the love of God. Let this chapter nourish you as you focus on love.

Mrs. T

. . . I clearly remember feeling God's presence surrounding me

Although I have been going to church on Sunday every week since I was a toddler, and even attending a religious school since kindergarten, only recently have I truly come to recognize and appreciate God's love in my life. While walking home from the bus stop about two years ago, I remember deciding to take the more scenic route through the woods back to my house. It was on that warm spring afternoon that I clearly remember feeling God's presence surrounding me. The warm sun on my face, the sweet breeze rustling the trees and the birds chirping nearby filled me with a sense of peace, warmth and joy that was none other than God's amazing love. From that day on, God's love has been a large part of my everyday life, and most importantly, my decision making.

Seeing God and His presence in all of creation, especially my family, friends, teachers and even complete strangers, has caused me to take a second look at how I treat others. Also, now, every time I am about to make an important decision, whether it's contemplating whether to go to a party where I know drinking will be prevalent or even just deciding what to buy for lunch, I ask myself which choice would be thanking God for His unwavering love. I have come to realize that appreciating God's love is probably one of the best ways to show Him how thankful I really am. Respecting others, ourselves and all of nature is a way everyone can feel God's love and show thanks. Besides clearly experiencing God's love through creation, I also believe that God's love is the warm feeling you experience after helping another individual. By realizing all beings are created in the image and likeness of God, when you help out another person in any way, you understand you are also sharing and professing your love for God. Therefore, as a result of God showering us with His love, we are able to discover this love within the core of our very beings.

Thea, 17

... God loves me even when everyone else seems not to care

God is love. When teenagers look at this phrase, we usually say, "Yeah, right." We don't believe in it because we have always been told that if we pray, God will always answer us and give us whatever we pray for. However, we don't realize that God grants us our petitions in many different ways. I don't consider myself an incredibly religious person. I believe in God, but I have lots of doubts about my faith. When something goes wrong, I blame the whole world for it; I blame God, too. But then there are times when everything *seems* to go wrong: I get in a fight with my parents and it seems like no one can help me. At these times I turn to God and just talk to Him. Sometimes I even go to church, and it just helps me get over my problems. When I sit in church, I feel safe and comfortable, and I know *that God is with me. Then no one is yelling at me; I am just sitting quietly thinking things over and over again, and I realize that God loves me even when everyone else seems not to care. I know then that with His help I can get over my problems much faster. Knowing that God always loves me helps me appreciate things and people around me, and this gives me confidence that He is always there for me no matter what happens.*

Jill, 17

I believe God has intentions for everyone . . .

Ever since I was a small girl, I have enjoyed the simple things. Being with my family, my brothers and my cousin is what I liked best. I enjoyed laughing with the people I loved and simply being with them. I know God is the being who put love on this Earth, and that without love we could not be. I believe God has intentions for everyone, and even though things may be bad at times, something is waiting for you. People who have faith in God are not the only ones who are loved. Everyone is, but sometimes things get in the way and we cannot see it. I know God will always be there for me, and no matter what, everyone can find love, and this love is what will make our lives complete.

Caroline, 18

I never asked God for His help . . .

In the past three years, I have had more worthwhile experiences than in the rest of my life put together. Along with new experiences, I have been influenced with new ideas and feelings from the people I am surrounded by. I have felt what it is to be a success and what it is to be a failure. I have known happiness and sadness, and I have known hope and despair. In the middle of all these feelings and experiences, I began to be confused about life in general. My freshman year I entered high school knowing only three people. I was scared I wouldn't be cool enough or smart enough or pretty enough to fit in with everyone. I tried so hard to be myself, but I often found myself acting differently just to be like everyone else.

This way of life continued during my sophomore and junior years. I would laugh at things I did not find funny. I agreed with things I did not believe in. I did just about anything to try to make others like me. I had a few close friends who I could be myself around, but in school or at parties I had to be careful how I acted. Oftentimes I would ask myself why I felt I had to be this way. Why couldn't I have been happy with who I was? I never asked God for His help during my time of need. I suppose I never really thought He would be any help to me. He was there the whole time, though, and I know that now.

In October of my senior year, I went on an overnight retreat. I was glad I got to miss two days of school, but I never expected it to have such an enormous impact on my life. My perspective on my family and friends, school and life in general was totally changed. I got in touch with God and myself in a way I never imagined was possible. I began to realize that in the past three years, I had not done anything for myself. Everything I ever did or said was for someone else. I finally realized that I did not have to do that. I know that my family will support me in anything that I choose to do with my life. I know who my true friends are, and they are all I need. I don't regret the past few years because I learned from all my mistakes. When I wasn't even looking for God, I found Him. I know that He will remain in my heart and love me forever. He is a powerful guiding force, and I feel fortunate to have realized it.

Shayne, 18

God's love is that unseen,
but not unfelt, presence . . .

God so loves the world that He gave Jesus, His son, to us. God gives unconditional love to all people, regardless of what they have or have not done. God's love is visible in all of nature, the birds, the trees, the sunshine. God's love is that unseen, but not unfelt, presence that makes the world a better place.

José, 17

My dad was an alcoholic . . .

I never really had a good relationship with God when I was younger, probably because He wasn't introduced to me by my parents. My dad was an alcoholic. He used to drink while he was at work and then come home and be very violent. My brother and I used to sit through the horrible fights every night, and it would usually get to the point where we (my mother, brother and I) had to leave and go get a hotel room. If you asked me two years ago how many nights I actually slept in my own bed, the answer would probably be no more than ten. Sometimes, my mom wouldn't leave the house and I would call a family friend. She would have to come and get us. I honestly believe this person is an angel in disguise. Through her, I began to have a relationship with God. She introduced me to Him and kept me headed in the right direction, even though all I was seeing was violence. Through her, God kept love in my heart instead of hate. He also gave me the strength to persevere. I know now that God has been with me every step of the way. My dad and mom divorced, which was for the best in our situation, and my dad finally got the help he needed. I wouldn't want anyone to go through what I have, but maybe with the love God has given me, someday I can use my experiences to help other people.

Roslyn, 14

AUTHOR'S NOTE: Please remember that should violence ever occur in your home, it is imperative to seek help. Talk to someone that you trust who can lead you to resources to keep you safe. At the same time, if you are ever in immediate danger, call 911 without hesitation, for the protection of yourself and your family. Also, keep in mind that if you are living with an addict, organizations such as Al-Anon or Alateen (1-888-4-AL-ANON/1-888-425-2666) can be helpful in providing support and guidance.

I guess God can sort of be considered the first eternal optimist . . .

We humans, with our faulty conscience and moral failings, have screwed up so many times you probably think God would have just washed His hands of us a while ago. He didn't, though, and probably never will. Can you understand that kind of patience and love? I mean, I can get pretty mad at small occurrences, never mind a world war or any other numerous instances where the human race has been less than perfect. I mean, can you imagine how stupid and misguided war must seem to God? Thousands of His supposedly intelligent creatures blowing each other's heads off for what? A chunk of land or a couple more meaningless pieces of paper or bars of yellow metal? Individually, we do rely heavily on God's patience and love. Sad as it may seem, if I tally up my day's actions, the ones

I perform are usually done more for bad intentions or wrong ones. But I haven't been struck down yet, so I guess God is willing to forgive me and keep His unshaking patience. I guess God can sort of be considered the first eternal optimist. He is always ready to forgive us (if we are ready to admit our fault) and is never negative in His view of our wavering world.

Hector, 17

I was a rebel child . . .

My life has been moderately hard. I think many teens would say the same about their lives. But I have not always lived my life the way I do now. I used to make very bad decisions. I used to cuss like a banshee. I used to all-out rebel and disrespect my mother. I was a rebel child, and I did not live my life in a way acceptable to God. And during all this time, if you asked me, "Are you a Christian?" I would have said yes. But I think that I would have been wrong. I've learned that you cannot just talk the talk; it is also important to walk the walk. I think that it was my youth group leader who helped me realize this.

My youth pastor took me directly under his wing and treated me like his son. He had a very strong belief about never cussing, as did the youth group. I feel that this is valid in that it can *stunt your spiritual growth. The Bible says, "From the overflow of the heart, the mouth speaks," and I did not want such disgusting things in my heart. Now I rarely ever cuss. My youth pastor also showed me unconditional love, which after a month or two I picked up on and started to attempt to treat others the way he treated me. It really isn't all that hard, I found, if you try. He taught me how to make right decisions by going to God and asking for His advice and always listening to His voice. If anything, this is one of the more difficult things for teens to do. He also showed me verses in the Bible about disrespecting your parents. He taught me how to deal with my parents and how to love them. That carried over to how I treated other people. If there is one thing I have always had trouble with, it is the command to "love all." What a command! How can you love people who treat you badly? I can tell you the answer to that. It is impossible for us to attempt to love all people on our own. You have to give it to God! He will give you the love in your heart to spread to all others. Then He will give you patience, love, kindness, selflessness and compassion, all of which I have found you need to love all others. Even though people are very cruel to me at times, even though*

I may not like them in the least, I will always try to love them. There are many times that I find that I cannot do some of these demanding tasks, and I have found that those are the times I am trying to do it on my own. You always have to give it to God. That doesn't mean you don't have to do some work in your life; it just means He will give you the power to do that work.

Bryan, 15

His love for each of us
is beyond comprehension . . .

I know that God is always there for me, waiting for me to speak to Him. He wants me to tell
Him anything, everything! I can pray to God at
any time. During the day, I find myself praying
for guidance whenever I need it. If I need a listening ear, I know He will be there for me. After
I pray, I am careful to stop for a few minutes
and listen for an answer. God will answer your
prayers! His love for each of us is beyond comprehension. When I feel this love, it surrounds
me like a blanket and I am peaceful inside.
Nothing else matters. I put all my trust in God,
and He showers me with unconditional love in
return. It's a great system. In this day and age,
it's easy to get pulled into the pressures of society. My faith in God keeps me steadfast on my
journey to eternal life in His presence. It's a

great feeling, being loved. With God on my side, I know that I am never alone.

Karson, 14

My life is very hard, but . . .

Sometimes things in my life become completely overwhelming, and there seems to be nowhere to turn. Things get so bad and lonely, I feel as though no one would notice if I was gone. On days like these, the only place I have to turn is to God. I am forced to think about the value of my life, knowing that God has given me so much. God gave me gifts; gifts I have to offer to other people. God has made me a strong person with all of my battles. My life is very hard, but someone out there has it worse. After every problem, it gets better. It helps me keep my faith.

I have to trust in God. I haven't given up on me, and though many other people think I am too messed up, God won't give up on me either. I know that I have respect, faith and trust in God, so He must have those things in me. No matter how hard my life gets, I will always have *someone to turn to, someone who loves me. Even in my days when I feel so completely worthless, I know that God is watching over me. And I know I can't give in. God gave me my life as a gift from Him, so I have to respect it. God gave me something, something of His own, and even though I feel like some days His choice for my life was unfair, I know by choosing this path for me I will have a better life, full of lessons and truths sent from God. So I have to believe and respect the gift He has given me. He gave me a life where I know people's struggles, I know what pain is, and I can be a person to offer comfort to the people who don't have the faith that I do. My life has given me such a greater respect for people and how they live, act and learn. God has a greater plan for me, and I can't give up, or I would be giving up on God and His love for me. Besides, I find great hope in knowing that someone will always love me: God!*

Jordan, 15

... God is carrying me in His loving arms

My relationship with God has shown me that I can depend on Him for guidance. As a stressed-out, confused teenager, I go through some weighted trials, even if most of it is on the inside. But I know that God can guide me and show me how to make sense of the chaos that can be pretty overbearing. I put my faith in Him and pray to God, because I know He is always there for me. When I am troubled and confused, I sometimes think of that "Footprints" poem, and how in my worst moments, God is carrying me in His loving arms.

Tino, 16

. . . I got so involved in drugs that nothing else mattered to me

Growing up has been difficult in my life. I haven't always had faith in God or in any religion . . . that is what is special about my story. It started when I was younger. I always hung out with older people, following them and sharing their beliefs. This made a huge impact on me as a young teen when my friends started using drugs. I shared their beliefs, and their beliefs were that there was nothing wrong with using drugs and staying out late. This affected me in a huge way, because I did everything that my peers did. If they wanted to get brain-dead by using mind-altering drugs, then at the time, there was absolutely no stopping me from doing it, too. I can admit that back then I had no faith at all in God. I didn't believe in the greatest man who could help me and eventually did help me: the Lord.

During that time, I got so involved in drugs that nothing else mattered to me. I didn't care about anything, including myself. Then, when I was at my lowest, the greatest thing happened in my life. God sent me someone who made me realize that I needed to get help. I didn't realize it at first, but God also sent me the best gift I could have: love. This love gave me a mind of my own and helped me to make decisions on my own. I started to realize and understand that through this gift from God, He had saved me. Since then I have accepted God as my personal savior. I know that as long as I keep Him in my life, even though it may not always be easy, I can get through anything. The Lord is always by my side and He will be for you, too, if you choose to believe.

Johnny, 16

AUTHOR'S NOTE: You can find help for a drug problem at the following numbers: National Youth Crisis Hotline (1-800-HIT-HOME/1-800-448-4663) and National Drug Abuse Hotline (1-800-662-4357).

...they carried out God's love

Comfort, help and friendship are all aspects of God's love. At one point in my life, confusion and pain were the only feelings that I endured. The death of my brother, whom I was closer to than anyone else on this Earth, destroyed my senses of reality and understanding. His death left me an emotional and psychological mess. At first, a sense of betrayal was all that I felt towards God. But that soon changed. Almost instantly after my brother died, friends began offering themselves to my family and me. These acts of kindness, compassion and love really helped me, not to understand, but to accept and grow. Friends from my church best represent God to me. I feel that they carried out God's love. By showing compassion and love through these people, God touched my heart and helped me heal.

Aarron, 17

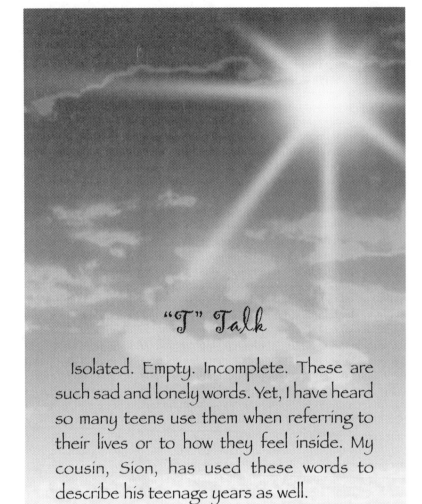

"J" Talk

Isolated. Empty. Incomplete. These are such sad and lonely words. Yet, I have heard so many teens use them when referring to their lives or to how they feel inside. My cousin, Sion, has used these words to describe his teenage years as well.

Although, if you were to ask Sion's peers, they likely would have told you that he had the ideal life, because when they looked at Sion's family and his lifestyle, they thought he had it all. They watched Sion's stepmom cheer louder and longer than anyone else at every one of Sion's football games. They knew that Sion's dad was one of the few who would give his son a big bear hug in front of everyone and say, "I love you." His friends were aware that Sion had a nice home, a hot car and a little extra spending money. They also knew that Sion's family spent time together on fun vacations, snowboarding, water-skiing and taking houseboat trips.

But what Sion's peers didn't see was that his biological mom and dad were both recovering addicts. They divorced when Sion was a child. Sion's dad remarried an extraordinary woman and together they did their best to raise Sion and his younger brothers with love and understanding.

Yet for Sion, something was still missing. Perhaps it was the addiction issues that had plagued his family throughout his childhood. Or he thinks it could have had something to do with the deaths of his best friends in a car accident—a car in which Sion was supposed to be riding. Regardless of the reason, an emptiness grew inside his heart. In his early teens, Sion chose to fill that void with temporary pleasures. He began to drink and experiment with drugs. Pot became Sion's drug of choice. Soon he was getting high every day, throughout the day. Even knowing that he was at risk for becoming an addict because of his family's history with addiction,

Sion still chose to use. In spite of knowing better, Sion also rationalized his use by telling himself that pot wasn't a hardcore drug. So he smoked a lot, slept a lot, and in between tried to maintain a some-what "normal" teen existence. The reality of the situation, however, was that as much as using alco-hol and drugs may have given Sion momentary plea-sure, the feeling never lasted.

It was not until recently, when Sion discovered God's unending love, that he realized that his short-lived vices were meaningless. He had gone to church in the past, and he had always believed in God; how-ever, his prior spiritual experiences had been rou-tine and insignificant. For some reason, even unbeknownst to Sion, this time it was different. It may have been something the pastor said, or per-haps it was simply that Sion was tired of living life as he was, but this time he experienced the feeling of his heart overflowing with the unconditional love of God. Only in that moment did he understand that the path he had chosen previously only nourished his feeling of emptiness. When Sion smoked pot, he could fill his lungs with smoke and hold it there until he began to feel the high taking hold. This high may have carried him a few moments or even a few hours, but now Sion understands that God's love can carry him for a lifetime. God's love is unconditional. He loves without reservation or restriction, despite one's faults or flaws. His love is unchanging, everlasting and pure. Can you imagine this type of love? Picture this:

A teenager goes to a party with his friends. His intention is to hang out, have fun and stay sober. However, everyone is having such a good time that when a beer is offered to him, he decides, "Why not?" Ultimately, that one beer turns into many more. Soon he knows that he's gone too far. His dad had always said that although he hoped his son would never put himself in such a situation, if he ever did, his dad would be only a phone call away. So the teen calls home and asks his dad to come pick him up. He waits nervously, worried that his dad will be mad and ground him 24/7, but more than that the teen fears that he will disappoint his dad. Yet, when his father arrives, he puts his arm around his son and walks him to the car. Once inside, the teen drops his head in his hands and with tears in his eyes says, "Dad, I'm so sorry. I don't know what I was thinking." His dad reaches over and touches his face so that their eyes meet, and he says, "Son, I love you so much. Even though I may not approve of your drinking tonight, I am proud that you called me."

Can you conceive the amount of love and grace that filled the car that night? Not to mention the abundance of love that was felt in each of their hearts. I find it amazing to consider that if a mortal father can love his child that much, then our heavenly Father is capable of a love beyond our wildest dreams! From a teen perspective, I would think that God's love would be one of the most incredible experiences in the world.

Because God's love is offered without strings attached, He loves you for who you are, not how you look or what you do. God loves you regardless of whether your hair is dyed or if you have a tattoo or a belly-button piercing. Likewise, He doesn't require that you wear certain clothes or shoes to be accepted by Him. Name brands mean nothing to God. He doesn't love you because you get good grades or because you are a fantastic musician or a great skater. You see, who you are on the outside doesn't matter to God. He loves you because of who you are on the inside. God loves you because you are YOU!

Given such, I have spoken with numerous teenagers who have expressed that they feel unworthy of God's love. Please know that no one is worthless in God's eyes. This is why He sent Jesus to live among us and die for us. It is also why He gave us the Holy Spirit to live within each of us. God's love for us is that strong. Rely on faith to connect your desire for a love so real with the blessing of God's offering. Open your heart to God, and let Him fill you with His love.

Considering God's gift of love to us, wouldn't you think that we should love one another in kind? The obvious answer would seem to be simple, yet the reality is quite bleak. Think about your school environment. There is so much judgment and jealousy that exists at most schools. Teens are labeled based on the way they dress, what they are involved in or where they live. People tease and discriminate on the premise of what someone looks like or who they hang out with. Sadly, no love can be found in this behavior. Consequently, the ultimate outcome causes heartache and anger and can force the judged into depression, isolation or rebellion. Where is the love in this? Why must we judge? Aren't we all similar on the inside? Don't we all crave love and understanding? Don't we all wrestle with our emotions when faced with difficult life situations? If so, then why not focus on love?

If you are thinking, "Yeah, why not?" then we should probably attempt to understand the meaning of love. Many would describe love as an emotion that one feels. Being "in love" may actually be described as a stronger emotion that makes your heart feel as if it is going to burst from the sheer pleasure and overwhelming joy that encompasses the feeling. At the same time, apostle Paul proposes that true love is fundamentally an action rather than an emotion. He writes, in essence, that if you were to use the model of Christ's love, you would be kind and patient. You would not be jealous or envious of others. If you were to act out of pure love, you would not be rude or conceited. Therefore, boasting would definitely be out. You would need to hold your temper and not keep track of the wrongs done to you. Your actions would always show honesty and truth. You would not do anything that would be considered evil or corrupt. You would always protect and trust people, including your parents. And you would always keep trying with a hopeful heart, even when utterly frustrated or confused.

I realize that it may seem almost impossible to even attempt to love others in such a way, especially on days when you wake up on the wrong side of the bed or get into a huge fight with your parents or friends. The good news is that God knows that you are going to have bad days. He understands your imperfections. After all, He created you. Who better to understand you than the Lord? So if you are confused or feeling inept about how to love others in such a Christlike way, take your concerns to God. Let Him guide you and teach you. Reflect on Jesus' model as the perfect example of how to love. During the days that Jesus walked the Earth, He was non-judgmental and accepting of all, especially those who were considered outcasts. He took time to meet the needs of others, but He also took care of Himself. If He needed time alone to pray, He made sure that His time was uninterrupted. In this way, He reminds us that acting out of love means loving our-selves as well. He also prayed for people with utter compassion and complete conviction. We, too, can love in this way. I feel sure that if we each take a step to love each other as God loves us, such love would enrich our family relationships, friendships and even our school atmosphere. For that matter, our world would flourish with love and peace.

On the other hand, you may feel that loving others comes naturally. Perhaps instead, you struggle with a need to be loved. Are you one who feels alone in this world? Do you ever wonder if any-one really cares about you? I know that I have spo-ken with many teens who have felt this way. Some have been homeless, others abused. Several felt neglected by parents who had to work long hours in order to put food on the table. There are numerous teenagers who feel unloved because their mom and dad have divorced, and now their parents' time and energy are focused on dating and making ends meet. This isn't to say that the parents of these teens don't love their kids, because undoubtedly they do; it is just that in their current situation, the teens may not *feel* loved. Regardless of why you might feel alone or unloved, know that God does love you. He is simply waiting for you to accept His love. Considering this, you may be wondering how to recognize God's love.

Remarkably, God showers us with His love in so many ways. When a stranger smiles at us and brightens our day, God's love is touching us through that person. When a friend shows us kindness, we can feel God's love. When we observe the beauty in nature, we can thank God for loving us so much to give us peace in the warm sun and hope in the majesty of the mountains. His love is even evident in joy that you feel in your heart when that hot girl or guy that you've been subtly flirting with all week flirts back. (Okay, so maybe your hormones have something to do with that one, but still.) When it comes down to it, God showers us with these visions and experiences so that we may have evidence of how much He cares.

With God's love will come a joy and fulfillment that you may have never felt before. If you have already accepted God's love in your life, then you know what I mean. My cousin Sion told me that when he first experienced God's love, he learned that there was a difference between happiness and joy. He found happiness to be temporary. A person can easily be happy one moment and sad the next. However, joy is eternal. It lives in your heart through God's love and stays forever. I pray that you find joy in God's love, because the power of His love can change the world. I encourage you to embrace, share and celebrate the love of the Lord!

CHAPTER TEN

Let Me Share
Your Hope

God is hope . . .

Throughout this book, you have read about the life experiences of a multitude of teens. They have taken you on a journey of their trials and tragedies, joys and triumphs. Some of the stories that you read may have touched your heart and brought tears to your eyes. Others might have made you smile or laugh. At the same time, I hope that many passages taught you lessons and encouraged you in your faith. But when it is all said and done, it comes down to this chapter. I say this because no matter what you experience in life, if you look to the Lord, He will grant hope to your heart every day! As teens will express in this final chapter, God is hope, and He desires to share it with you!

Mrs. T

God's love is never ending . . .

Ever had a constant romance in your life, and then all of a sudden the romance ends and you are left in the dust? How do you feel? Do you feel angry, betrayed, alone? Well, there is one who will never leave you alone. When you think no one cares about you or even loves you, you are wrong. There is one who loves you with all of His heart and will never forsake you, ever! His name is Jesus, and over two thousand years ago He walked this Earth, died, was nailed to a cross and was resurrected just to save someone like YOU. To you, that may sound way too extreme. And it might scare you in some ways, but He died to give you life. As the scripture John 3:16 says: "For God so loved the world that He gave His only son that whoever believes in Him shall not perish but have everlasting life." God's love is never ending. If you don't know God, please find a church, talk to a pastor or ask a friend who does know God for help. I assure you that they will help you meet God. Please take advantage of this glorious miracle and embrace the love that is waiting for you in God's arms!

Wrenna, 15

He gave us life, so why not believe . . .

I believe in God for many reasons. He can help us so much. Ever since day one, I have had faith in God and each year it grows stronger. If I somehow got pulled away from Him, I would be blind and lost. He will help anyone, if you just ask Him with sincerity. He loves us all and He wants to help us. He gave us life, so why not believe in Him? When I am scared, nervous or faced with a hard decision, I turn to Him and He leads me in the right direction. Not only do I ask for His guidance in those situations, but I do it every day. Sometimes I just ask Him to keep me strong, so I can resist the temptations of the world. He has always been there for me, and I know that He will be there for you if you just ask Him.

Alice, 14

Having faith is like a shining light...

Life without faith? I don't even want to think about it. It's like living in an empty void with nothing around you but space. Having faith is like a shining light. It is a glimmer of hope worth striving for. It helps us reach our goals and dreams. It helps us be the true person that we really want to be. Faith is one of the greatest things you can have in life. It's a shame if you do not have it.

Akeem, 18

God is everything you need . . .

Everyone has a "God is. . . ." It is as unique as each person's perception. What is important to being a complete person is finding out what God is in your life. What God is to you will depend on your life experiences and present situation. God is a guiding force, a confidant and a conscience. God is forgiving and understanding. God is everything you need because to you God is . . . ?

Tamera, 17

You can let Him in by opening your heart . . .

God will help anyone at any time. He doesn't judge your past, but wants you to have a good future. He also provides you with the hope that He will guide you out of troubles or misfortunes. He will do this because He loves you, and if you let Him in, He will do anything for you. You can let Him in by opening your heart to Him, not asking for things, but thanking Him for being present in your life. If you just acknowledge Him, He will help you and provide hope for your life.

Corey, 15

He will always be there . . .

It's really hard for me to tell you why I am a Christian. It is not just a thing you do or say, but a way of life. It is indescribable. When you truly have Jesus as your Lord and Savior, you will never be alone again. You will never have to make a decision by yourself again. He will always be there for you. I know lots of people who think faith or religion is just a bunch of rules to live by, but it's not. It is more than that. It truly is a way to have love in your life by living every day of your life for God.

Grace, 14

*I want to be what
He wants me to be . . .*

As I look to the heavens I know He is there,
Showering me, giving me His love and all of His
  care.
Every day I wake up and thank God for life,
He's helped me through so much, all of my pain
  and my strife.

I feel God inside me; I know He is there to show
  me the way,
To guide me, to love me, to help me through
  every single day.
Jesus is there above me, and I thank Him for all
  He has done.
He is the Savior, the Messiah; it is my heart that
  He has won.

The emotions and feelings I have for God are too strong to express in words.

He has shown me the world and has given me life; the true things that matter from Him I have learned.

I want to be what He wants me to be; it is Jesus that I see.

I get down on my knees and pray thanks that my Lord loves me.

I have my faith, oh Lord, and it comes straight from my heart.

It is this faith in you that from my body shall never part.

And I say to you, Lord, that no matter what happens, no matter what I do,

I hope you are listening, oh Lord, because God, I love you!

Antonio, 16

My faith in God has given me a sense of direction and hope . . .

Teenage years are probably some of the most difficult times to go through. There is peer pressure to do things that may not appeal to you, there is the fear of what people might think of you if you don't fit in, and there is a great amount of confusion about friendships and relationships. Although things sometimes seem so hard, I have learned through experience that if you have hope in God and believe that He will guide you through things, it will be okay. I realize through my faith in God that even in the toughest times, I know that someone else in the world has it worse than me and that I should be happy for what God did give me and learn to accept my hardships. My faith in God has given me a sense of direction and hope. It has taught me to stand strong in my beliefs and values, and *not worry about what others think because God is the one who truly knows me. So stay positive towards your own values, and your hope in God will help you through.*

Dani, 16

He is the little light of hope . . .

God is always there with you. He is the little light of hope getting you through the worst days of your life.

Mayson, 18

My poem to God . . .

When I didn't know who to go to
You were there with an open heart
And all the times that I was confused
You showed me a way out of the dark
All the times that I was hurt and
Tears filled up in my eyes
You told me I don't have to be strong
All the time and that it's okay to cry
Every problem that came along
You were there to help me through it
Every time I was nervous
You made me feel like I could do it
How can I give back to You what
You have done for me
Now that I have Your guidance
Now that I do believe
Every time that I am scared
I can always believe

Because now I know that You are here
And You will never leave

Mike, 15

. . . remember that your number-one supporter is God

God wants you to be humble, healthy and smart. But this doesn't mean that those of you who aren't humble or healthy, or don't make smart decisions, are not loved by God. God loves everybody, even if you have sex when you're young, do drugs, drink or have an addiction. If you do these things, you may be hurting yourself and others around you. You may even need help to stop. But you need to remember that your number-one supporter is God.

The truth is, He knows that there is a part of you that screams, "Faith, I need it!" Instead, you might deny yourself and scream, "Drugs or sex! I need more." That's how people block the shame and guilt, depression and anger. But it's God who lets you feel these things. If you believe in God, He can guide you out of the hole that you may have dug yourself into. Nobody is unworthy of God's love. I used to feel like that, so I became inactive at church and turned into a stranger. I wasn't happy with myself, so I lied, lied and lied. Everyone who knew me saw that I was going down the wrong path. I got into trouble, cheated and got into arguments with my parents. I became depressed. I tried to change, but I could never stop lying. In fact, I lied more than ever. I put on an act that I was "Miss Perfect." I tried hanging out with different groups. Then I started to hang around the "quiet, yet smarts." They had a really good influence on me. They brought the inside, the true me, out. And hey, I wasn't that bad. I started going back to church and praying. I became more mature. And you know what? It was God who helped me, loved me and was there right by my side the whole time. Guess what? I don't lie anymore. So don't let yourself get down. God will always be there to help you, too!

Jennifer, 14

*. . . God will always wait for us
to turn back to Him . . .*

Bad things happen all the time. Every day,
every minute and every second something bad is
happening. That seems so negative to me, but it
is the truth in the world today. There are times
that people feel that they can do nothing and
turn away from God. When people turn away
from God, God waits for them. He is kind of like
an old friend who people can go back to when
they need to. This privilege can be misused as
well, but God will always wait for us to turn
back to Him, because of His undying and unconditional love for us. When people have had a
death in the family, drug problems or suicidal
thoughts, they may turn their backs on God, but
hopefully they will realize what they are doing
and will turn back to Him. He has always been
there for us, and He always will be.

Tess, 16

. . . God will always forgive you . . .

I know how much God helps me every day, and I want people, including you, to have the same feeling that I do . . . that someone cares for you, that you have someone to talk to when you're feeling bad. The Lord is always there for you, and He loves you and forgives you even when you sin. In Psalm 23 it says: "The Lord is my shepherd. . . . He restores my soul." I think the psalm means that God will always forgive you, and He will restore your mind and soul with good, not bad. If you already are a Christian, I just have one more thing to say: Share the Lord with people, and let them see His light through you and how happy you are to have the Lord in your life!

Angelice, 14

. . . God helped me through . . . the death of my brother

I was always brought up as a Christian. When I was born, my mom was a strong Christian and still is. I went to church with her as much as possible. When I was old enough to understand completely, I accepted God as my personal Lord and Savior. He has helped me through many things. The one specific event that God helped me through the most was the death of my brother. I mean, I still feel the pain of losing my only brother, but God reminds me that He has a plan for everything and that we will be reunited in heaven someday. God keeps me on the right path. When I am presented with a difficult situation, I go directly to Him. He guides me, just like a lost sheep. I rely on Him for everything, because without God, we are nothing.

So, what would I tell teens about Him? I would

have to start by telling them that He can help you through all your problems—anything from relationships, school, family, friends, etc. Also, He will give you eternal life in heaven if you would just believe in Him. People say that Christians miss out on all the good things . . . drinking, sex, all the fun. But I don't think so; by setting standards, God is just protecting you and that just shows that He cares very deeply for you.

Jay, 15

God loves all of us, no matter who we are or what we've done . . .

God is the most powerful being ever to exist. He has created all that you have ever seen, and much more. He was always there, and He will always be there. For anyone. God loves all of us, no matter who we are or what we've done. He created us. He knows us. God is important to me because He is there when I need Him, whether it be His courage, strength or wisdom. God will always help anyone in need, as long as they ask for it. He can, and will, help you with your school work, friendships or difficult decisions in your life. Anything. He is God, and He will help by filling your life with His presence. He will also help you through tough times in your life. If you have accepted God, and you've committed several sins in your life, He'll still love you just as much. He is a forgiving God, and He cares *about you. All you need to do is accept Him and let Him into your heart.*

Robert, 14

. . . *I am saved* . . .

Has anyone ever told you how great God is? Well, God is GREAT!! He is a strong and loving Father. He is the best. I believe in God because through this belief, I know that I am saved because of Jesus Christ, God's only son. Faith is like a bridge between me and God. If I didn't have faith, it would be like not having air. My faith is a part of who I am. I am shaped around it. I am who I am because of what I believe. I believe in God, my only and everlasting Father; Jesus, my savior and everlasting friend; the Holy Spirit, my leader and everlasting guide. I am a Christian. I hope that you can believe in God, too!

Benita, 16

. . . a wonderful feeling of peace . . .

I can't really pick out or define one specific area or category of God that means the most to me. He's been so involved in every single aspect of my life, especially recently. My life has been definitely better, more rich and joyful since I've decided to let God in. First off, I guess, is guidance. My junior year has been extremely stressful, and sometimes I have trouble handling it. My anxiety bubbles over into other areas in my life, and my friends, family and relationships always suffer. For a while, I might even get confused about God. Then something always happens to make it better. Maybe a song comes on the radio or a friend calls or a teacher spends a little extra time with me. Or even, for no reason at all, a wonderful feeling of peace comes over me. At times like this, I know God is guiding me and comforting me, saying, "It's going to be all right, don't worry."

God has an awesome amount of patience, too. The number of times I've messed up or turned my back on Him is countless. Yet, there's always His love, beckoning me back. Because of this, I've realized that all of my guilt and sin can be washed away by God's love and patience. It's an awesome gift.

This sort of leads into my next point: God is grace. I feel so overwhelmed at times, and all of a sudden, I can literally feel His loving presence. And that's what grace is, God's forgiving and patient presence. If His grace is with you, you're okay. One time, I did some pretty bad stuff. I thought that I had hidden it pretty well from my parents, but I hadn't. They found out, and I was busted. My punishment was severe, but it fit the offense. However, I was inconsolable. All of these thoughts ran through my mind: "I'm a rotten kid," "Why am I even here?" "I'm a waste of air," and "Nobody will ever trust me again." Basically, I was wallowing in self-pity. Then, I could suddenly sense this feeling of peacefulness, and I knew it was God's grace healing and consoling me.

When I was little, I used to say my prayers every night, regarding them more as an obligation than anything else. Then I started to realize what prayer is: not reciting rote passages as fast as you can so you won't go to hell, but being with God, hanging out with Him, if you will. I think over this last year, I've prayed more than ever before, in both ways, ritual and conversation. I've learned that God will answer your prayers. It might not always be in the way that you want, but God does listen and respond to you. All of these things I've talked about have one thing in common: my faith in God. It's central to everything in my life. I know that with Him, I can do anything. Like that church song goes: "If God is for us, who can be against us?" Give God a shot in your life. What have you got to lose?

Travis, 16

Actions definitely speak louder than words . . .

All my life I have been raised a Christian. I have always gone to a religious school, and I attend church regularly. When compared to the society around me, I always considered myself to be a pretty devoted Christian. That view of myself drastically changed six months ago when I spent three weeks of my summer in a little village way up in the mountains of Haiti. In the village of Dessables, the people have virtually no material possessions, especially when compared to the environment I am accustomed to. Their houses are made of sticks, and they are lucky if they have an animal or two. Sometimes they will not eat for a week. Yet these people have incredible faith in God. The feeling you get when you are there in this presence is indescribable. I could truly see the face of God when I looked at these people. No matter what, they always put people before anything else. And even though we didn't speak the same language, I could always understand them. Actions definitely speak louder than words. They would go to church for the entire day on Sunday. And it is so full of life. Even though they didn't know where their next meal was coming from, they put their faith in God to watch over them. This experience has given me the strength to go beyond what is expected of me in my society as a Christian. I think of these people, and I know that I am doing good things, even when people question me as to why I put so much time and effort into God. It is not just for Him, but also for me and all people of the world. I share this experience with you, hoping that you can see these people as an example and grow in your faith, too.

Kailyn, 17

God will send His Holy Spirit to you . . .

Did you know that God's love for you is stronger than any human love that you can imagine? To Him, you are precious, and He loves you unconditionally—despite all your faults and the bad things you may have done. God loved you so much that He gave His one and only son to die for you on a cross. Jesus did not have to die such a death, but He did—because He wanted you to live with Him forever in heaven. Jesus bought you with a price—His own blood. If you only believe this, you will be a child of God. All you need to do is let Jesus be the Lord and master of your life. God will send His Holy Spirit to you so that you will be filled with it and have great faith in the Lord. Reading the Bible will strengthen your faith a lot. A good place to start is the gospel of Luke. (If you don't have a Bible,

*there should be one at a nearby public library.)
Praying to God will also strengthen your faith in
Him. If you are not a Christian, going to church
may make it easier to find Christianity. When
you're a Christian, you will find comfort and
strength in God. You can rely on Him because He
will always be there for you!*

Genna, 13

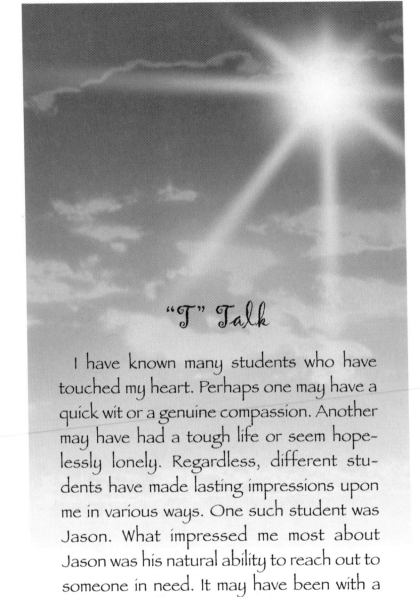

"J" Talk

I have known many students who have touched my heart. Perhaps one may have a quick wit or a genuine compassion. Another may have had a tough life or seem hopelessly lonely. Regardless, different students have made lasting impressions upon me in various ways. One such student was Jason. What impressed me most about Jason was his natural ability to reach out to someone in need. It may have been with a touch, a smile or even with a particular action. Jason always took it upon himself to look after others. However, after getting to know Jason, I realized that although he took initiative when it came to helping out his peers, he didn't seem to take time for himself. I asked him about it once, and he said that as far as he was concerned, his life really didn't matter. Jason told me about his parents' divorce, and how he'd like to live with his dad. However, in addition to his dad's verbally abusive behavior, he didn't seem to want Jason in his life. Jason explained that his relationship with his mom and siblings was falling apart. Jason felt that no one in his family listened to him or seemed to care about what he thought. This made him either depressed or extremely angry. He felt that he had no control over either of these feelings. To compound these emotions, Jason's best friend had recently died and his girlfriend was in the process of being diagnosed with cancer. In his grief, his fear for her health and his frustration within his own family, Jason felt that he had no one to turn to.

Eventually, Jason confided in me that he felt an overwhelming sense of hopelessness. Feeling a bit helpless myself at the gravity of his situation, I asked him two questions. The first was if he would be open to counseling. He said that he'd tried that, but at this point didn't want to pursue counseling. Second, I asked Jason if he had a spiritual faith to turn to during this difficult time in his life. Considering that he felt he had no one who would understand or listen to him, I thought that if he could turn to God, he wouldn't feel so alone. Yet, Jason wasn't so sure. He wondered if there really was a God, then why didn't He do something to show Jason that He cared? Why didn't He make Jason's life better? I asked Jason to consider that sometimes when we feel so discouraged or helpless, that is the perfect time to open our hearts to hope.

I remember leaving that conversation with Jason, wishing that he could see that if only he could find faith in God, he would discover hope in his life, for I truly believe that our time on this Earth is a spiritual journey. I believe that everything that we experience in some way enhances our spiritual growth. That doesn't mean that God wants bad things to happen. But at the same time, I think that when bad things happen in our lives, God can enlighten us with precious life lessons, if only we would choose to open our hearts to His teachings. Perhaps if Jason could understand this, he wouldn't feel so disheartened.

Hope. I talk to teens every day who have lost hope. Perhaps they have experienced a trial or tragedy in their lives, like some of the kids who wrote for this book. Maybe they have been abused or neglected. Perhaps someone in their lives died senselessly. More likely, though, the reason is a temporary problem that overwhelms them, like a breakup with a girlfriend or boyfriend or an inability to communicate with their parents. Yet regardless of the situation, a sense of hopelessness prevails. As Jason eventually discovered, though, the Lord can guide you out of your deepest despair.

To my surprise and answered prayers, that very summer Jason discovered God, and through his newfound faith, he encountered hope. Jason wrote me a letter that summer, telling me that he had been spending most of his time supporting his girlfriend through her radiation treatments. Yet, Jason had a different perspective this time. He said that he credited his new outlook to his girlfriend and her faith, and ultimately to God. Jason wrote, "I look at God, and I thank Him every day for the faith that He has given me and my girlfriend. The reason I have faith is because she had it and I finally caught on. Having faith is like having this feeling in you that helps you know everything will be okay in the end." Jason told me that as he stood by his girlfriend throughout her time in the hospital, he had felt so much hope. He knew that she would beat the disease. At the same time, he understood that we all have obstacles that we have to deal with in life. However, he felt that he would be able confront those placed upon his path, because finding faith in God had led him to faith in himself. Jason didn't feel hopeless anymore. In fact, he said that if I were to ask him what the word "faith" means to him now, he would say that it means power—the power to be able to take yourself out of situations that are hard and make them a little bit easier. Jason could not have done this alone, but with God by his side he felt that anything was possible.

If you are a Christian, you are probably smiling right now because you can identify with Jason. What a glorious feeling it is to share one's faith in the Lord. When your emptiness has been filled with God's love, when your doubt has been turned to belief by the Lord's comfort, you want other people to experience this feeling, too. Remember, though, that it is important to share God's hope without judging people for their resistance or skepticism. The best way to lead people to the Lord is with acceptance and love. Show them, by your actions, the peace and hope that they, too, can discover in Christianity. Be conscientious of their hesitation or doubt. If they seem to be pushing you away or avoiding you, it is possible that you are coming on too strong. Sometimes an overzealous Christian ends up alienating the very people he or she is trying to lead to Christ. Keep in mind that if you keep a humble heart and focus on

God's love, He will guide you and help you to witness in a way that glorifies Him.

If you do not consider yourself a Christian or if you are trying to figure out this whole "God thing," know that discovery is part of your life journey. God is patiently knocking on the door to your heart. He doesn't have any desire to leave His place there, because that is where He belongs. His sole purpose is to be available for you, to be yours. But, He will not enter without an invitation. He wants the choice to be yours. Does that mean that if you invite Him in, you will hear fireworks and immediately feel "saved"? Maybe, but probably not. I can't tell you what you'll feel, because everyone's experience is unique. God touches each person's heart in a special way. Some people need time to get used to God living there and loving there. Others are ready to jump into a relationship with God right away. Regardless, I'll bet that if nothing else, you will feel just a tiny bit of peace enter your heart. God's promise to you is that, like a mustard seed growing, peace will grow into strength, love and hope that exemplifies the glorious life found in the kingdom of God.

You may be wondering exactly how the Lord might provide someone with hope. I suppose He does so in a myriad of ways. Some teens have told me that feeling Christ's comforting presence has brought them peace. Others, like my friend Laura, have experienced a true miracle. Keep in mind that miracles are not beyond God's mighty power, and miracles undoubtedly bring hope. Many teenagers have shared that they discovered hope in an answered prayer. On the other hand, sometimes hope is found in an answer that is entirely different than we expected. Nonetheless, if you let God reside in your heart, a glimmer of hope will abide in endless splendor.

Still, I have had many teenagers say to me that they don't know how to invite God in; they don't know how to ask Him. The beauty of it is that there isn't a right or wrong way. You can simply use your own words to tell God that you want to turn your life over to Him. Ask God to reveal Himself to you in a way that you will understand. Tell Him that you want to love Him and receive His love in return. In your own words, express your sorrow for your past mis-deeds and ask Him to guide you in your words and actions in the future. God will be so happy that you are opening your heart to Him that how you went about doing it will not matter to God at all.

Remember that when you feel you have nothing, you always have God. Sometimes, especially as teenagers, we are so focused on ourselves and our needs that it is difficult to let go of the hold we have on our problems and our lives and grab on to hope of God's love. Yet if you choose to let God hold you, your life will be lighter. There will be room in your heart for the Lord's joy. He is the Comforter and the Provider. He is the Maker and Counselor. God is the Lord of hope and the Giver of peace. If you don't have the answers and you are looking for hope, rely on the Lord. However, like Jason discovered, it is a matter of choice. You can turn from God, but in doing so you will be turning from His ability to provide you with the hope to persevere. So turn towards Him, and let God fill you with hope while you experience His joy, peace, courage and love!

Note to the Reader

Dear Reader,

I hope that *Teens Talkin' Faith* has touched your heart and inspired your soul. I believe that God was present throughout the writing of this book, and that He is present with you now. Please turn to Him for guidance; rely on Him for hope. You are surely worth His love!

I wrote and compiled *Teens Talkin' Faith* because I believed that it would make a difference in your life. My prayer was that this book would renew and reinforce your established faith or help lead you to a new and everlasting relationship with God. If *Teens Talkin' Faith* has affected you in such a way, I would love to hear about it! Please write me via my Web site at

www.teenstalkinfaith.com

Also, if you are interested in contributing your perspective to future books, I would be pleased to accept your submission. I am pursuing topics specific to grief and loss, suicide, peer pressure and living with disabilities. I am also interested in your personal experience with miracles or angels. You can find more information on my *teenstalkinfaith.com* Web site.

If you have never read my first book, *Why Can't We Talk? What Teens Would Share If Parents Would Listen,* I encourage you to do so. It will help you to know that you are not alone in the situations you experience as a teen. It also can be a powerful tool that will help you to communicate with your parents in that you can read a passage that you identify with and then share it with your parents so that they might come to understand you better. For more information on this book, or to schedule me for a speaking presentation or training, check out

www.whycantwetalk.com

Thank you and God bless!

                                        Mrs. T

Appendix I
Scriptural References
(New International Version)

I have included several scriptural passages that apply to the general content areas of *Teen Talkin' Faith*, but the Bible is literally full of encouraging and enlightening verses. I encourage you to take time to explore the word of God on your own!

Mrs. T

DOUBT

Deuteronomy 31:8

The Lord Himself goes before you and will be with you; He will never leave you nor forsake you.

James 1:6

But when He asks, he must believe and not doubt, because he who doubts is like a wave of the sea, blown and tossed by the wind.

Hebrews 11:1

Faith is being sure of what we hope for and certain of what we do not see.

Hebrews 13:5–6

Keep your lives free from the love of money and be content with what you have, because God has said, "Never will I leave you; never will I forsake you." So we say with confidence, "The Lord is my helper; I will not be afraid. What can man do to me?"

John 20:26–29

A week later His disciples were in the house again, and Thomas was with them. Though the doors were locked, Jesus came and stood among them and said, "Peace be with you!" Then He said to Thomas, "Put your finger here; see my hands. Reach out your hand and put it into my side. Stop doubting and believe." Thomas said to Him, "My Lord and my God!" Then Jesus told him, "Because you have seen me, you have believed; blessed are those who have not seen and yet have believed."

Matthew 14:22–33

Immediately, Jesus made the disciples get into the boat and go on ahead of Him to the other side, while He dismissed the crowd. After He had dismissed them, He went up on a mountainside by Himself to pray. When evening came, He was there alone, but the boat was already a considerable distance from land, buffeted by the waves because the wind was against it. During the fourth watch of the night, Jesus went out to them, walking on the lake. When the disciples saw Him walking on the lake, they were terrified. "It's a ghost," they said, and cried out in fear. But Jesus immediately said to them: "Take courage!

It is I. Don't be afraid." "Lord, if it's you," Peter replied, "tell me to come to you on the water." "Come," He said. Then Peter got down out of the boat, walked on the water and came toward Jesus. But when he saw the wind, he was afraid and, beginning to sink, cried out, "Lord, save me!" Immediately, Jesus reached out His hand and caught him. "You of little faith," He said, "why did you doubt?" And when they climbed into the boat, the wind died down. Then those who were in the boat worshiped Him, saying, "Truly You are the Son of God."

2 Corinthians 5:7

We live by faith, not by sight.

Mark 9:23

"Everything is possible for him who believes."

Isaiah 55:8–9

"For my thoughts are not your thoughts, neither are your ways my ways," declares the Lord. "As the heavens are higher than the Earth, so are my ways higher than your ways and my thoughts than your thoughts."

Romans 5:3–5

Not only so, but we also rejoice in our sufferings, because we know that suffering produces perseverance; perseverance, character; and character, hope. And hope does not disappoint us, because God has poured out His love into our hearts by the Holy Spirit, whom He has given us.

COURAGE AND STRENGTH

Hebrews 13:6

So we say with confidence, "The Lord is my helper; I will not be afraid. What can man do to me?"

Psalm 3:3–4

But You are a shield around me, O Lord; You bestow glory on me and lift up my head. To the Lord I cry aloud, and He answers me from His holy hill.

Psalm 18:6

In my distress I called to the Lord; I cried to my God for help. From His temple He heard my voice; my cry came before Him, into His ears.

Psalm 27:14

Wait for the Lord; be strong and take heart and wait for the Lord.

Psalm 31:3

Since You are my rock and my fortress, for the sake of Your name lead and guide me.

Psalm 118:6

The Lord is with me; I will not be afraid.

Psalm 119:28

My soul is weary with sorrow; strengthen me according to Your word.

Isaiah 12:2

Surely God is my salvation; I will trust and not be afraid. The Lord, the Lord, is my strength and my song; He has become my salvation.

Isaiah 41:13

For I am the Lord, your God, who takes hold of your right hand and says to you, do not fear; I will help you.

Romans 5:3–5

Not only so, but we also rejoice in our sufferings, because we know that suffering produces perseverance; perseverance, character; and character, hope. And hope does not disappoint us, because God has poured out His love into our hearts by the Holy Spirit, whom He has given us.

Philippians 4:13

I can do everything through Him who gives me strength.

Ephesians 6:10–11

Finally, be strong in the Lord and in His mighty power. Put on the full armor of God so that you can take your stand against the devil's schemes.

1 Corinthians 16:13–14

Be on your guard; stand firm in the faith; be men of courage; be strong. Do everything in love.

2 Corinthians 12:10

That is why, for Christ's sake, I delight in weaknesses, in insults, in hardships, in persecutions, in difficulties. For when I am weak, then I am strong.

FORGIVENESS

Matthew 18:21–22

Then Peter came to Jesus and asked, "Lord, how many times shall I forgive my brother when he sins against me? Up to seven times?" Jesus answered, "I tell you, not seven times, but seventy-seven times."

Colossians 2:13–14

When you are dead in your sins and in the uncircumcision of your sinful nature, God made you alive with Christ. He forgave us all our sins, having canceled the written code, with its regulations, that was against us and that stood opposed to us; He took it away, nailing it to the cross.

Ephesians 1:7–8

In Him we have redemption through His blood, the forgiveness of sins, in accordance with the riches of God's grace that He lavished on us with all wisdom and understanding.

Ephesians 4:32

Be kind and compassionate to one another, forgiving each other, just as in Christ God forgave you.

Romans 6:14

For sin shall not be your master, because you are not under law, but under grace.

Romans 8:8–9

Those controlled by the sinful nature cannot please God. You, however, are controlled not by the sinful nature, but by the Spirit.

2 Corinthians 5:17

Therefore, if anyone is in Christ, he is a new creation; the old has gone, the new has come!

Psalm 103:12

As far as the East is from the West, so far has He removed our transgressions from us.

Daniel 9:9

The Lord our God is merciful and forgiving, even though we have rebelled against Him.

Mark 11:25

And when you stand praying, if you hold anything against anyone, forgive him, so that your Father in heaven may forgive you your sins.

Luke 6:37

Do not judge, and you will not be judged. Do not condemn, and you will not be condemned. Forgive, and you will be forgiven.

Psalm 51:2

Wash away all my iniquity and cleanse me from my sin.

1 John 1:9

If we confess our sins, He is faithful and just and will forgive us our sins and purify us from all unrighteousness.

ANGER

Psalm 37:8

Refrain from anger and turn from wrath; do not fret—it leads only to evil.

Psalm 103:8–9

The Lord is compassionate and gracious, slow to anger, abounding in love. He will not always accuse, nor will He harbor His anger forever.

Proverbs 3:5–6

Trust in the Lord with all your heart and lean not on your own understanding; in all your ways acknowledge Him, and He will make your paths straight.

Proverbs 15:1

A gentle answer turns away wrath, but a harsh word stirs up anger.

1 Peter 4:12–13

Dear friends, do not be surprised at the painful trial you are suffering, as though something strange were happening to you. But rejoice that you participate in the sufferings of Christ, so that you may be overjoyed when His glory is revealed.

1 Corinthians 13:5

[Love] is not rude, it is not self-seeking, it is not easily angered, it keeps no record of wrongs.

Matthew 6:14

For if you forgive men when they sin against you, your heavenly Father will also forgive you.

Ephesians 4:26

"In your anger do not sin": Do not let the sun go down while you are still angry.

James 1:19–20

My dear brothers, take note of this: Everyone should be quick to listen, slow to speak and slow to become angry, for man's anger does not bring about the righteous life that God desires.

TRUST

Proverbs 3:5–6

Trust in the Lord with all your heart and lean not on your own understanding; in all your ways acknowledge Him and He will make your paths straight.

Proverbs 22:17–19

Pay attention and listen to the sayings of the wise; apply your heart to what I teach, for it is pleasing when you keep them in your heart and have all of them ready on your lips. So that your trust may be in the Lord, I teach you today, even you.

Hebrews 13:5

"Never will I leave you; never will I forsake you."

Psalm 27:14

Wait for the Lord; be strong and take heart and wait for the Lord.

Psalm 37:5–6

Commit your way to the Lord; trust Him and He will do this: He will make your righteousness shine like the dawn, the justice of your cause like the noonday sun.

Psalm 125:1

Those who trust in the Lord are like Mount Zion, which cannot be shaken but endures forever.

Isaiah 50:10

Who among you fears the Lord and obeys the word of His servant? Let him who walks in the dark, who has no light, trust in the name of the Lord and rely on his God.

Isaiah 58:11

The Lord will guide you always; He will satisfy your needs in the sun-scorched land and will strengthen your frame. You will be like a well-watered garden, like a spring whose waters never fail.

John 14:1–2

Do not let your hearts be troubled. Trust in God; trust also in me. In my Father's house are many rooms; if it were not so, I would have told you. I am going there to prepare a place for you.

PRAYER

1 Thessalonians 5:16–18

Be joyful always; pray continually; give thanks in all circumstances, for this is God's will for you in Christ Jesus.

Colossians 4:2

Devote yourselves to prayer, being watchful and thankful.

James 4:8

Come near to God and He will come near to you.

Job 22:27

You will pray to Him, and He will hear you, and you will fulfill your vows.

Psalm 91:14–15

"Because he loves me," says the Lord, "I will rescue him; I will protect him, for he acknowledges my name. He will call upon me, and I will answer him; I will be with him in trouble, I will deliver him and honor him."

Psalm 145:18

The Lord is near to all who call on Him, to all who call on Him in truth.

Matthew 6:9–13

Jesus said, "This, then, is how you should pray: 'Our Father in heaven, hallowed be Your name, Your kingdom come, your will be done on Earth as it is in heaven. Give us today our daily bread. Forgive us our debts, as we also have forgiven our debtors. And lead us not into temptation, but deliver us from the evil one.'"

Matthew 7:7–8

"Ask and it will be given to you; seek and you will find; knock and the door will be opened to you. For everyone who asks receives; he who seeks finds; and to him who knocks, the door will be opened."

Matthew 18:19–20

"Again, I tell you that if two of you on Earth agree about anything you ask for, it will be done for you by my Father in heaven. For where two or three come together in my name, there am I with them."

Philippians 4:6–7

Do not be anxious about anything, but in everything, by prayer and petition, with thanksgiving, present your requests to God. And the peace of God, which transcends all understanding, will guard your hearts and your minds in Christ Jesus.

Romans 12:12

Be joyful in hope, patient in affliction, faithful in prayer.

Mark 1:35

Very early in the morning, while it was still dark, Jesus got up, left the house and went off to a solitary place, where He prayed.

LOVE

1 John 4:7–8

Let us love one another, for love comes from God. Everyone who loves has been born of God and knows God. Whoever does not love does not know God, because God is love.

1 Thessalonians 3:12

May the Lord make your love increase and overflow for each other and for everyone else.

1 Corinthians 13:4–7

Love is patient, love is kind. It does not envy, it does not boast, it is not proud. It is not rude, it is not self-seeking, it is not easily angered, it keeps no record of wrongs. Love does not delight in evil but rejoices with the truth. It always protects, always trusts, always hopes, always perseveres.

John 3:16

For God so loved the world that He gave His one and only Son, that whoever believes in Him shall not perish, but have eternal life.

John 13:34

"A new command I give you: Love one another. As I have loved you, so you must love one another."

Deuteronomy 6:5

Love the Lord your God with all your heart and with all your soul and with all your strength.

Galatians 5:6

The only thing that counts is faith expressing itself through love.

Philippians 1:9–11

And this is my prayer: that your love may abound more and more in knowledge and depth of insight, so that you may be able to discern what is best and may be pure and blameless until the day of Christ, filled with the fruit of righteousness that comes through Jesus Christ—to the glory and praise of God.

Ephesians 3:16–19

I pray that out of His glorious riches He may strengthen you with power through His Spirit in your inner being, so that Christ may dwell in your hearts through faith. And I pray that you, being rooted and established in love, may have power, together with all the saints, to grasp how wide and long and high and deep is the love of Christ, and to know this love that surpasses knowledge—that you may be filled to the measure of all the fullness of God.

Ephesians 4:2

Be completely humble and gentle; be patient, bearing with one another in love.

FAITH AND HOPE

Romans 10:17

Faith comes from hearing the message, and the message is heard through the word of Christ.

Hebrews 6:19–20

We have this hope as an anchor for the soul, firm and secure. It enters the inner sanctuary behind the curtain, where Jesus, who went before us, has entered on our behalf.

Hebrews 11:3

By faith we understand that the universe was formed at God's command, so that what is seen was not made out of what was visible.

2 Corinthians 5:7

We live by faith, not by sight.

Ephesians 3:12

In Christ and through faith in Christ we may approach God with freedom and confidence.

Micah 7:7

But as for me, I watch in hope for the Lord, I wait for God my Savior; my God will hear me.

Isaiah 40:31

But those who hope in the Lord will renew their strength. They will soar on wings like eagles; they will run and not grow weary, they will walk and not be faint.

Philippians 4:7

And the peace of God, which transcends all understanding, will guard your hearts and your minds in Christ Jesus.

Romans 5:3–5

Not only so, but we also rejoice in our sufferings, because we know that suffering produces perseverance; perseverance, character; and character, hope. And hope does not disappoint us, because God has poured out His love into our hearts by the Holy Spirit, whom he has given us.

Romans 12:12

Be joyful in hope, patient in affliction, faithful in prayer.

Philemon 1:6

I pray that you may be active in sharing your faith, so that you will have a full understanding of every good thing we have in Christ.

$\mathscr{A}$ppendix II
$\mathscr{R}$esources and $\mathscr{H}$otlines

Christian-Based Teen Helplines and Web Sites:

National Youth Crisis Hotline: 1-800-HIT-HOME (1-800-448-4663)

A gospel-oriented hotline, from Youth Development International, for youth in crisis situations including physical abuse, rape, runaways, pregnancy, drug use and addiction, functioning with the purpose of restoring hope and the truth of Jesus Christ to American youth.

Youth Ministry Yellow Pages: *www.youthworkers.net*
Resources and referrals for Christian teens.

Cook Ministries: *www.cookministries.com*
Custom Discipleship and other Cook resources provide the tools necessary for teens to become more like Christ.

Rockettown, Inc.: *www.rockettown.com* or 1-615-843-4001 (outreach office)
Christian-based organization founded by Michael W. Smith and his wife, Debbie. Provides troubled teens

healthy after-school and evening activities. Tennessee-based, soon to be nationwide.

The Covenant House: *www.covenanthouse.org* or 1-800-388-3888
An agency that provides shelter and service to homeless and runaway youth

General Teen Helplines, Information Lines and Web Sites:

Al-Anon/Alateen: 1-800-356-9996 or 1-888-4-AL-ANON (1-888-425-2666)

Alcoholics Anonymous: See National Clearinghouse for Alcohol and Drug Information for a toll-free number or *www.aa.org.*

Eating Disorders Awareness and Prevention, Information and Referral Line: 1-800-931-2237

Grief Recovery Helpline: 1-800-445-4808

Narcotics Anonymous: See National Clearinghouse for Alcohol and Drug Information for a toll-free number or *www.na.org.*

National Clearinghouse for Alcohol and Drug Information: 1-800-788-2800
Will provide toll-free numbers for Alcoholics Anonymous and Narcotics Anonymous specific to the state in which one resides, as well as other toll-free numbers related to addiction issues.

National Clearinghouse on Child Abuse and Neglect: 1-800-394-3366

National Council on Alcoholism and Drug Dependence: 1-800-622-2255

National Directory of Children, Youth and Family Services: 1-800-343-6681

National Drug Abuse Hotline: 1-800-662-4357

National Health Information Center: 1-800-336-4797

National Referral Network for Kids in Crisis: 1-800-KID-SAVE (1-800-543-7283)

National Referral Organization for Drug/Alcohol Treatment Programs: 1-800-454-8966

National Resource Center on Domestic Violence: 1-800-537-2238

National Runaway Switchboard: 1-800-621-4000

National Suicide Hotline: 1-800-SUICIDE (1-800-784-2433)

National Youth Crisis Hotline: 1-800-HIT-HOME (1-800-448-4663)

Rape, Abuse and Incest National Network (RAINN): 1-800-656-HOPE (1-800-656-4673)

Yellow Ribbon Foundation (Suicide Foundation): *www.yellowribbon.org*